Verse 2

  C   F C
Hark, a voice from yonder manger,

    Dm7 G7 C
Soft and sweet, doth entreat,

 G   D7 G
"Flee from woe and danger.

 Dm   Dm7   G7 C
Brethren, come from all grieves you.

   G7   C
You are freed; all you need

 C7 Dm7 G7 C
I will surely give you."

Verse 3

  C   F C
Come then, let us hasten yonder.

    Dm7 G   C
Here let all,___ great and small,

 G   D7 G
Kneel in awe and wonder.

 Dm   Dm7   G7 C
Love Him who with love is yearning.

    G   C
Hail the star that from far

 C7   Dm7 G7 C
Bright with hope is burning.

Angels from the Realms of Glory

Words by James Montgomery
Music by Henry T. Smart

Melody:

An - gels   from   the...

C   F   G7   E   Am   G   D7   C7   Dm

Verse 1

C
Angels from the realms of glory,

F   **C**   **G7**   **C**
Wing your flight o'er all the earth;

                    E
Ye who sang creation's story,

Am   **G** **D7** **G**
Now proclaim Mes - si - ah's birth.

Chorus 1

G7
Come and worship!

C7   **F**
Come and worship!

Dm   **G7**   **C**
Worship Christ the newborn King!

UKULELE CHORD SONGBOOK

Christmas
Carols

ISBN 978-1-4584-1100-6

HAL•LEONARD®
CORPORATION
7777 W. BLUEMOUND RD. P.O. BOX 13819 MILWAUKEE, WI 53213

In Australia Contact:
Hal Leonard Australia Pty. Ltd.
4 Lentara Court
Cheltenham, Victoria, 3192 Australia
Email: ausadmin@halleonard.com.au

Visit Hal Leonard Online at
www.halleonard.com

Ukulele Chord Songbook

Contents

All My Heart This Night Rejoices

Words by Paul Gerhardt
Translated by Catherine Winkworth
Traditional Music

Melody:

All my heart this...

Verse 1

       C   F   C
All my heart this night rejoices,

     Dm7 G7   C
As I hear, far and near,

    G   D7 G
Sweetest angel voices.

    Dm   Dm7   G7   C
"Christ is born," their choirs are singing,

          G   C
Till the air ev'rywhere

    C7   Dm7 G7 C
Now with joy is ringing.

UKULELE CHORD SONGBOOK

Verse 2

C
Shepherds in the fields abiding,

F   C   G7   C
Watching o'er your flocks by night,

                  E
God with man is now residing;

Am   G D7 G
Yonder shines the in - fant Light.

Chorus 2   *Repeat Chorus 1*

Verse 3

C
Sages, leave your contemplations,

F   C   G7   C
Brighter visions beam a - far,

                  E
Seek the great Desire of nations,

Am   G D7 G
Ye have seen His natal star.

Chorus 3   *Repeat Chorus 1*

Verse 4

C
Saints before the altar bending,

F   C   G7   C
Watching long in hope and fear,

                  E
Suddenly the Lord, descending,

Am   G   D7 G
In His temple shall ap - pear.

Chorus 4   *Repeat Chorus 1*

Angels We Have Heard on High

Traditional French Carol
Translated by James Chadwick

Melody:

An - gels   we   have...

G   D   D7   E   Am   C

132   233   1113   2331   2   3

Verse 1

      G   **D**   **G**
Angels we have heard on high,

              D7   **G**
Singing sweetly o'er the plains,

               D   **G**
And the mountains in reply

             D7   **G**
Echoing their joyous strains.

Chorus 1

G **E** **Am** **D** **G** **C** **D7**
Glo - -   -   -   - - ria.

G   **D**
In excelsis Deo,

G **E** **Am** **D** **G** **C** **D7**
Glo - -   -   -   - - ria.

G   **D7** **G**
In excelsis De - o.

UKULELE CHORD SONGBOOK

Verse 2

         G   D   G
Shepherds, why this jubilee?

                D7   G
Why your joyous strains prolong?

                D   G
What the gladsome tidings be

                D7   G
Which inspire your heavenly song?

Chorus 2

Repeat Chorus 1

Verse 3

         G   D   G
Come to Bethlehem and see

                D7   G
Him whose birth the angels sing.

                D   G
Come adore on bended knee

                D7   G
Christ the Lord, the newborn King.

Chorus 3

Repeat Chorus 1

Verse 4

         G   D   G
See within a manger laid

                D7   G
Jesus, Lord of heav'n and earth!

                D   G
Mary, Joseph, lend your aid;

                D7   G
With us sing our Savior's birth.

Chorus 4

Repeat Chorus 1

As with Gladness Men of Old

Words by William Chatterton Dix
Music by Conrad Kocher

Melody:

As with ___ glad - ness...

G	D	C	D7
1 3 2	2 3 3	3	1 1 1 3

Verse 1

    G   D   G   C   D7 G
As with gladness men of old

C   G C D   G
Did the guiding star behold;

        D G   C   D7 G
As with joy they hailed its light,

C   G C   D   G
Leading onward, beaming bright;

             D   G
So, most gracious Lord, may we

C G   C G D G
Evermore be led to Thee.

Verse 2

    G   D G C   D7 G
As with joyful steps they sped

C   G C D   G
To that lowly manger bed,

        D   G   C   D7 G
There to bend the knee before

C   G   C   D   G
Him whom heav'n and earth adore;

             D   G
So may we with willing feet

C G   C G D G
Ever seek thy mercy seat.

Verse 3

G   D   G   C   D7   G
As they of - fered gifts most rare

C   G   C   D   G
At that manger rude and bare;

D   G   C D7 G
So may we with holy joy,

C   G   C   D   G
Pure and free from sin's alloy,

D   G
All our costliest treasures bring,

C   G   C   G   D G
Christ, to Thee, our heav'nly King.

Verse 4

G   D G   C D7 G
Holy Jesus, ev'ry day

C   G C   D   G
Keep us in the narrow way;

D   G   C   D7   G
And when earthly things are past,

C   G   C   D   G
Bring our ransomed souls at last

D   G
Where they need no star to guide,

C   G   C   G D G
Where no clouds Thy glory hide.

Away in a Manger

Words by John T. McFarland (v.3)
Music by James R. Murray

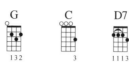

Verse 1

G   C G
Away in a manger, no crib for His bed,
  D7   G
The little Lord Jesus lay down His sweet head;
          C   G
The stars in the bright sky looked down where He lay,
  D7 G C   D7 G
The little Lord Jesus, asleep in the hay.

Verse 2

      G   C G
The cattle are lowing, the baby awakes,
  D7   G
But little Lord Jesus no crying He makes.
           C   G
I love Thee, Lord Jesus! Look down from the sky,
  D7 G C D7 G
And stay by my side until morning is nigh.

Verse 3

      G   C   G
Be near me, Lord Jesus; I ask Thee to stay
  D7   G
Close by me forever, and love me, I pray.
         C   G
Bless all the dear children in Thy tender care,
  D7 G C   D7 G
And take us to heaven, to live with Thee there.

Bring a Torch, Jeannette, Isabella

17th Century French Provençal Carol

Melody:

Bring a torch... _

G   Am   D   D7   C   Em

Verse 1

G   Am   D
Bring a torch, Jeannette, Isa - bella,

G   D7   G
Bring a torch, come swiftly and run.

                                                D
Christ is born, tell the folk of the village,

C   G   D7   G D
Jesus is sleeping in His cradle,

Em D G   D   G
Ah, ah, beautiful is the Mother,

Em D G   D   G
Ah, ah, beautiful is her Son.

Verse 2

G   Am   D
Hasten now, good folk of the village,

G   D7   G
Hasten now, the Christ Child to see.

                                                D
You will find Him asleep in a manger,

C   G   D7   G D
Quietly come and whisper softly,

Em   D   G   D   G
Hush, hush, peacefully now He slumbers,

Em   D   G   D   G
Hush, hush, peacefully now He sleeps.

A Child Is Born in Bethlehem

14th-Century Latin Text adapted by Nicolai F.S. Grundtvig
Traditional Danish Melody

Melody:

G   D   D7   Am   C

132   233   1112   2   3

Verse 1

G
A Child is born in Bethlehem,

D G   D7 G
In Beth - le - hem;

Am G   D Am G C
And joy is in Je - ru - sa - lem,

D G   Am G D7 G
Alleluja, Al - le - lu - ja!

Verse 2

G
A lowly maiden all alone,

D G D7 G
So all a - lone,

Am G   D Am G C
Gave birth to God's own Ho - ly Son.

D G   Am G D7 G
Alleluja, Al - le - lu - ja!

Verse 3

G
She chose a manger for His bed,

D G D7 G
For Jesus' bed.

Am   G   D AmG C
God's angels sang for joy o'erhead,

D G   Am G D7 G
Alleluja, Al - le - lu - ja!

Verse 4

G
Give thanks and praise eternally,

D G   D7 G
E - ter - nal - ly,

AmG   D Am G C
To God, the Holy Trin - i - ty.

D G   Am G D7 G
Alleluja, Al - le - lu - ja!

Child Jesus

Words by Hans Christian Andersen
Music by Niels Gade

Child Je - sus in a...

Verse 1

      C G   C G D
Child Jesus in a manger lay,

G   C Am G D G
Yet Heaven was His own.____

     C G   C G D
His lowly pillow was of straw,

G D   Em Bm F♯   Bm
And 'round Him no light shone._____

D G   D E Am D G
But Heaven sent a star so bright,

        C   B   Em
And oxen kissed His feet that night,

C D Em F♯ Bm
Alleluja, Alleluja,

Em C D G
Al - le - lu - ja!

Verse 2

C G   C G D
O crippled soul be glad today,

G   C Am G D G
Cast out your bit - ter pain.____

C G   C G D
For Bethle'm's Babe will show the way,

G D Em Bm F$\sharp$ Bm
We heav'nly bliss can gain._____

D G   D E Am D G
Let us with child-like heart and mind,

C   B   Em
Seek now the Son of God to find.

C D Em F$\sharp$ Bm
Alleluja, Alleluja,

Em C D G
Al - le - lu - ja!

Christ Was Born on Christmas Day

Traditional

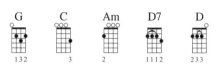

G   C   Am   D7   D

Verse

```
    G                    C  G
Christ was born on Christmas Day,

                      C  G
Wreath the holly, twine the bay;

Am    D7   G  D
Christus natus hodie;

      G      C      G  D7    G
The Babe, the Son, the Holy One of Mary.
```

The First Noël

17th Century English Carol
Music from W. Sandys' *Christmas Carols*

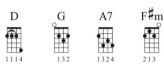

```
1114        132        1324       213
```

Verse 1

      D   G   D
The first Noël, the angel did say,

      G   D   A7   D
Was to certain poor shepherds in fields as they lay;

      G   D
In fields where they lay keeping their sheep,

      G   D   A7 D
On a cold winter's night that was so deep.

Chorus 1

      D   F#m   G   D
Noël, No - ël,___ No - ël,___ No - ël,

      G   A7   D A7 D
Born is the King of Is - ra - el.

Verse 2

      D   G   D
They looked up and saw a star

      G   D   A7   D
Shining in the East, beyond them far;

      G   D
And to the earth it gave great light,

      G   D   A7   D
And so it continued both day and night.

Chorus 2   *Repeat Chorus 1*

Verse 3

```
            D          G       D
And by the light of that same star,

      G       D        A7     D
Three wise men came from country far;

            G          D
To seek for a King was their intent,

      G       D        A7     D
And to follow the star wherever it went.
```

Chorus 3   *Repeat Chorus 1*

Verse 4

```
            D              G       D
This star drew nigh to the northwest,

    G     D    A7     D
O'er Bethlehem it took its rest;

              G          D
And there it did both stop and stay,

      G       D          A7    D
Right over the place where Jesus lay.
```

Chorus 4   *Repeat Chorus 1*

Verse 5

      D   G   D
Then entered in those wise men three,

    G   D   A7   D
Full reverently upon their knee;

                 G   D
And offered there in His presence,

    G   D   A7   D
Their gold, and myrrh, and frankincense.

Chorus 5   *Repeat Chorus 1*

Verse 6

      D   G   D
Then let us all with one accord

    G   D   A7   D
Sing praises to our heav'nly Lord,

              G   D
That hath made heav'n and earth of naught,

    G   D   A7   D
And with His blood mankind hath brought.

Chorus 6   *Repeat Chorus 1*

Coventry Carol

Words by Robert Croo
Traditional English Melody

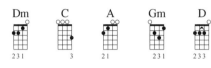

Verse 1

   Dm   **C** **A**
Lullay, thou little tiny Child,

Dm   **Gm Dm**
By by, lully lullay.

    C   **Gm A**
Lullay, thou little tiny Child,

Dm   **Gm D**
By by, lully lullay.

Verse 2

   Dm   **C**   **A**
O sisters too, how may we do,

Dm   **Gm**   **Dm**
For to preserve this day.

    C   **Gm**   **A**
This poor youngling for whom we sing,

Dm   **Gm D**
By by, lully lullay.

Verse 3

Dm   C   A
Herod the king, in his raging,

Dm   Gm   Dm
Charged he hath this day.

     C   Gm   A
His men of might, in his own sight,

Dm   Gm   D
All young children to slay.

Verse 4

Dm   C   A
That woe is me, poor Child for Thee!

Dm   Gm   Dm
And ever morn and day,

     C   Gm   A
For thy parting nor say nor sing,

Dm   Gm   D
By by, lully lullay.

Deck the Hall

Traditional Welsh Carol

F   C   Am   Dm   G7   B♭

Verse 1

F
Deck the hall with boughs of holly,

C   **F**   **C**   **F**
Fa la la la la, la la la la.

'Tis the season to be jolly,

C   **F**   **C**   **F**
Fa la la la la, la la la la.

C   **F**
Don we now our gay apparel,

Am   **Dm**   **G7**   **C**
Fa la la, la la la, la la la.

F
Troll the ancient Yuletide carol,

B♭   **F**   **C**   **F**
Fa la la la la, la la la la.

Verse 2

F
See the blazing yule before us,

C   F   C   F
Fa la la la la, la la la la.

Strike the harp and join the chorus,

C   F   C   F
Fa la la la la, la la la la.

C   F
Follow me in merry measure,

Am   Dm   G7   C
Fa la la, la la la, la la la.

F
While I tell of Yuletide treasure,

B♭   F   C   F
Fa la la la la, la la la la.

Verse 3

F
Fast away the old year passes,

C   F   C   F
Fa la la la la, la la la la.

Hail the new, ye lads and lasses,

C   F   C   F
Fa la la la la, la la la la.

C   F
Sing we joyous, all together,

Am   Dm   G7   C
Fa la la, la la la, la la la.

F
Heedless of the wind and weather,

B♭   F   C   F
Fa la la la la, la la la la.

Ding Dong! Merrily on High

French Carol

Melody:

Ding dong! Mer - ri - ly on   high...

Verse 1

    C   **D7**   **G7**
Ding dong! Merrily on high,

    F   **C**
In heav'n the bells are ringing.

         D7   **G7**
Ding dong! Verily the sky

    F   **C**
Is riv'n with angel singing.

Chorus 1

    Em **Am7** **Dm7** **G7**
Glo - - - -

    Em **Am** **Bm7♭5** **E7**
- - - - -

    Am **Dm7** **G7**
- - - - ria,

    F   **G7 C**
Hosanna in ex - celsis!

UKULELE CHORD SONGBOOK

Verse 2

    C   **D7**   **G7**
E'en so here below, be - low,

       F   **C**
Let steeple bells be swungen,

     D7   **G7**
And io, io, io,

     F   **C**
By priest and people sungen.

Chorus 2   *Repeat Chorus 1*

The Friendly Beasts

Traditional English Carol

Je - sus our broth - er,...

G   D7   C   Em   Am7

Verse 1

G D7 G   D7   G
Jesus our brother, kind and good,

        C   D7   G
Was humbly born in a stable rude,

        C   G D7   G
And the friendly beasts a - round Him stood,

    C G Em Am7 D7 G
Jesus our brother,__ kind and good.

Verse 2

G   D7 G   D7   G
"I," said the donkey, shaggy and brown,

       C   D7   G
"I carried His mother up hill and down;

      C   G D7   G
I carried her safely to Bethlehem town."

     C G Em Am7 D7 G
"I," said the donkey, shaggy and brown.

Verse 3

```
        G      D7 G       D7      G
"I," said the cow all white and red,

              C        D7    G
"I gave Him my manger for His bed;

            C   G D7       G
I gave Him my hay to pillow His head."

            C   G    Em Am7 D7 G
"I," said the cow all white and red.
```

Verse 4

```
   G      D7 G          D7  G
"I," said the sheep with curly horn,

              C         D7    G
"I gave Him my wool for His blanket warm;

          C    G D7       G
He wore my coat on Christmas morn."

          C  G      Em Am7  D7 G
"I," said the sheep with cur - ly  horn.
```

Verse 5

```
   G      D7 G            D7    G
"I," said the dove from the rafters high,

              C        D7       G
"I cooed Him to sleep so He would not cry;

              C    G D7      G
We cooed Him to sleep, my mate and I."

            C  G        Em Am7 D7 G
"I," said the dove from the raf - ters high.
```

Verse 6

```
   G      D7 G      D7         G
Thus every beast by some good spell,

           C       D7    G
In the stable dark was glad to tell

           C   G    D7      G
Of the gift he gave Em - man - u - el,

           C  G   Em  Am7 D7 G
The gift he gave Em - man - u - el.
```

From the Eastern Mountains

Words by Godfrey Thring
Traditional Melody

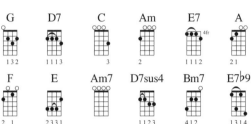

Verse 1

G   D7   G   D7
From the eastern mountains,

G   C   D7
Pressing on they come,

Am   E7   Am A
Wise men in their wis - dom,

G   D7   G
To His humble home.

          F   E E7
Stirred by deep de - vo - tion,

Am   Am7   D7sus4 D7
Hasting from a - far,_____

Am D7   Bm7 E7♭9
Ever journ'ing on - ward,

Am7 D7 G
Guided by a star.

Verse 2

G   D7   G D7
There their Lord and Savior

G   C   D7
Meek and lowly lay,

Am   E7   Am A
Wondrous light that led them

G   D7   G
Onward on their way.

     F   E E7
Ever now to lighten

Am   Am7   D7sus4 D7
Nations from a - far,_____

Am   D7   Bm7 E7♭9
As they journey homeward

Am7 D7   G
By that guiding star.

Verse 3

G   D7 G D7
Thou who in a manger

G   C   D7
Once hast lowly lain,

Am   E7   Am A
Who dost now in glo - ry

G   D7   G
O'er all kingdoms reign,

     F   E E7
Gather in the heathen

Am   Am7   D7sus4 D7
Who in lands a - far_____

Am   D7   Bm7 E7♭9
Ne'er have seen the brightness

Am7 D7   G
Of Thy guiding star.

Verse 4

    G   D7   G D7
Gather in the outcasts,

    G   C   D7
All who have a - stray,

    Am   E7   Am A
Throw Thy radiance o'er them,

    G   D7   G
Guide them on their way.

           F   E   E7
Those who never knew Thee,

    Am   Am7   D7sus4 D7
Those who have wandered far,_____

    Am   D7   Bm7 E7♭9
Guide them by the brightness

    Am7 D7   G
Of Thy guiding star.

Verse 5

    G   D7   G   D7
Onward through the darkness

    G   C   D7
Of the lonely night,

    Am   E7   Am A
Shining still be - fore them

    G   D7   G
With Thy kindly light.

           F   E E7
Guide them, Jew and Gentile,

    Am   Am7   D7sus4 D7
Homeward from a - far,_____

    Am   D7   Bm7 E7♭9
Young and old to - geth - er,

    Am7 D7   G
By Thy guiding star.

Good King Wenceslas

Words by John M. Neale
Music from *Piae Cantiones*

Verse 1

G
Good King Wenceslas looked out

C   D7   G
On the feast of Stephen,

When the snow lay round about,

C   D7   G
Deep and crisp and even;

    D7   G   Em
Brightly shone the moon that night,

C   D7   G
Though the frost was cruel,

    B7   Em   D7
When a poor man came in sight,

G   D7   G C G
Gath'ring winter fu - el.

Verse 2

G
"Hither, page, and stand by me,

C   D7   G
If thou know'st it, telling,

Yonder peasant, who is he?

C   D7   G
Where and what his dwelling?"

         D7   G   Em
"Sire, he lives a good league hence,

C   D7   G
Underneath the mountain;

         B7   Em D7
Right a - gainst the forest fence,

G   D7   G   C G
By Saint Agnes' foun   - tain."

Verse 3

G
"Bring me flesh and bring me wine,

C   D7   G
Bring me pine logs hither;

Thou and I will see him dine,

C   D7   G
When we bear them thither."

         D7   G   Em
Page and monarch, forth they went,

C   D7   G
Forth they went to - gether;

         B7   Em   D7
Through the rude wind's wild la - ment

G   D7   G C G
And the bitter weath - er.

Verse 4

G
"Sire, the night is darker now,

C   D7   G
And the wind blows stronger;

Fails my heart, I know not how,

C   D7 G
I can go no longer."

         D7   G   Em
"Mark my footsteps, my good page,

C   D7   G
Tread thou in them boldly;

         B7   Em   D7
Thou shalt find the winter's rage

G   D7   G C G
Freeze thy blood less cold - ly."

Verse 5

G
In his master's steps he trod,

C   D7   G
Where the snow lay dinted;

Heat was in the very sod

C   D7   G
Which the saint had printed.

         D7   G   Em
Therefore, Christian men, be sure,

C   D7   G
Wealth or rank pos - sessing,

         B7   Em   D7
Ye who now will bless the poor,

G   D7   G C G
Shall your - selves find bles - sing.

Fum, Fum, Fum

Traditional Catalonian Carol

Am   Dm   E7   C   G7   F

Verse 1

        Am   **Dm**   **E7**
On this joyful Christmas day

       Am   E7   Am
Sing fum, fum, fum.

         Dm   **E7**
On this joyful Christmas Day

       Am   E7   Am
Sing fum, fum, fum.

        C   **G7**   **C**
For a blessed Babe was born

              G7   **C**
Upon this day at break of morn.

     F   **Dm**   **E7**
In a manger poor and lowly

       Am   Dm   **E7**
Lay the Son of God most holy.

Am   E7   Am
Fum, fum, fum.

Verse 2

Am   Dm E7
Thanks to God for holidays,

    Am E7 Am
Sing fum, fum, fum.

            Dm E7
Thanks to God for holidays,

    Am E7 Am
Sing fum, fum, fum.

      C   G7   C
Now we all our voices raise

         G7   C
And sing a song of grateful praise,

    F   Dm   E7
Celebrate in song and story

    Am   Dm E7
All the wonders of His glory,

Am E7 Am
Fum, fum, fum.

Gather Around the Christmas Tree

By John H. Hopkins

Melody:

Gath - er a-round the   Christ-mas tree!...

G   D7   B7   Em   Am   D   A7   C

132   1112   321   3421   2   233   1324   3

Verse 1

```
       G              D7      G
Gather around the Christmas tree!

                D7      G
Gather around the Christmas tree!

    B7 Em          Am      D7
Ev - er green have its branches been,

    G       D  A7      D
It is king of all the woodland scene.

    D               B7       Em
For Christ, our king is born to - day,

    C               A7      D
His reign shall never pass a - way.
```

Chorus 1

```
G   C   D  G   C   D
Ho - san - na, Ho - san - na,

G   D7  Em  Am  G  D7  G
Ho - san - na__ in__ the highest!
```

Verse 2

```
G              D7      G
Gather around the Christmas tree!

               D7      G
Gather around the Christmas tree!

   B7 Em        Am      D7
Once the pride of the mountainside,

      G              D  A7      D
Now cut down to grace our Christmastide.

G  D                  B7        Em
For Christ from heav'n to earth came down

      C              A7      D
To gain, through death, a nobler crown.
```

Chorus 2   *Repeat Chorus 1*

Verse 3

```
G              D7      G
Gather around the Christmas tree!

               D7      G
Gather around the Christmas tree!

  B7 Em         Am      D7
Ev'ry bough has a burden now,

      G          D  A7    D
They are gifts of love for us, we trow.

G  D                  B7    Em
For Christ is born, his love to show

      C          A7   D
And give good gifts to men below.
```

Chorus 3   *Repeat Chorus 1*

Glad Christmas Bells

Traditional American Carol

Am7   D7   C7   B7   Em   G

1 1 1 2   1   3 2 1   3 4 2 1   1 3 2

Verse 1

   Am7 D7 C7 B7 Em
Glad Christmas bells, your music tells

   Am7 D7   G
The sweet and pleasant sto - ry,

    Am7 D7 C7 B7 Em
How came to earth, in lowly birth,

   Am7 D7   G
The Lord of life and glo - ry.

Verse 2

   Am7 D7 C7 B7 Em
No palace hall, its ceiling tall;

   Am7 D7   G
is kingly head spread o - ver,

    Am7 D7 C7 B7 Em
There only stood a_ table rude;

   Am7 D7   G
The heav'nly Babe to cov - er.

Verse 3

Am7   D7 C7 B7   Em
Nor raiment gay as there He lay,

Am7   D7   G
Adorn'd the infant stranger;

Am7   D7   C7 B7   Em
Poor humble child of mother mild

Am7   D7   G
She laid Him in a manger.

Verse 4

Am7   D7 C7 B7   Em
But from a - far, a_ splendid star;

Am7   D7   G
The wise men westward turning;

Am7   D7 C7 B7   Em
The livelong night saw pure and bright,

Am7   D7   G
A - bove His birthplace burning.

Go, Tell It on the Mountain

African-American Spiritual
Verses by John W. Work, Jr.

Melody:

Go tell it on the moun - tain,...

G	Am7	D7	Em	C	A7	D7sus4
1 3 2		1 1 1 3	3 4 2 1	3	1 3 2 4	1 1 2 3

Chorus 1

G
Go tell it on the mountain,

Am7   D7   G   D7
Over the hills and ev'rywhere;

G   Em
Go tell it on the mountain

   Am7 D7   G
That Jesus Christ is born.

Verse 1

   G
While shepherds kept their watching

   C   G
O'er silent flocks by night,

Behold, throughout the heavens,

   Em   A7 D7sus4 D7
There shone a holy light._____

Chorus 2   *Repeat Chorus 1*

Verse 2

G
The shepherds feared and trembled

    C   G
When, lo! above the earth

Rang out the angel chorus

    Em   A7   D7sus4 D7
That hailed our Savior's birth._____

Chorus 3   *Repeat Chorus 1*

Verse 3

G
Down in a lowly manger

    C   G
The humble Christ was born,

And God sent us salvation

    Em   A7   D7sus4 D7
That blessed Christmas morn._____

Chorus 4   *Repeat Chorus 1*

God Rest Ye Merry, Gentlemen

19th Century English Carol

Melody:

God rest ye mer - ry, gen - tle - men,...

Dm   A7   B♭   Gm   F   C

Verse 1

      Dm
God rest ye merry, gentlemen,

          A7
Let nothing you dismay,

    Dm
For Jesus Christ our Savior

    B♭   **A7**
Was born on upon this day,

    Gm   **F**
To save us all from Satan's power

     Dm   **C**
When we were gone a - stray.

Chorus 1

    F   **A7**   **Dm**
O tidings of comfort and joy,

         C
Comfort and joy;

    F   **A7**   **Dm**
O tidings of comfort and joy.

Verse 2

      Dm
In Bethlehem, in Jewry,

          A7
This blessed Babe was born,

      Dm
And laid within a manger

    Bb   **A7**
Up - on this blessed morn;

    Gm   **F**
To which His mother Mary

    Dm   **C**
Did nothing take in scorn.

Chorus 2   *Repeat Chorus 1*

Verse 3

      Dm
From God our Heav'nly Father,

      A7
A blessed Angel came;

    Dm
And unto certain shepherds

    Bb   **A7**
Brought tidings of the same;

    Gm   **F**
How that in Bethlehem was born

    Dm   **C**
The Son of God by Name.

Chorus 3   *Repeat Chorus 1*

Going to Bethlehem

Traditional Chilean Carol

Good eve - ning, dear, gen-tle Mar - y, _____

G   D7   C   D   A7   A

132   1112   3   233   1324   21

Verse 1

       G   D7
Good evening, dear, gentle Mary,

          G
My heart is filled with devotion,

          D7
My heart is filled with devotion.

        G
For you and Jesus so lovely,

          C
A fervent prayer I am off'ring,

    D A7   D
A fervent prayer I am off'ring.

Chorus 1

       G   D7
Going, going to Bethlehem town,

          G
Going, going the Baby to see.

         C
To greet His father, Joseph,

    D A7   D
And Mary, on bended knee.

Verse 2

$$\begin{array}{ll} \text{G} & \text{D7} \end{array}$$
Goodbye to you little Manuel,

G
Until the New Year beginning,

D7
Until the New Year beginning.

G
I'll see you after the shearing,

C
So rich from wool you'll be selling,

$$\begin{array}{lll} \text{D} & \text{A7} & \text{D} \end{array}$$
So rich from wool you'll be selling.

Chorus 2

Repeat Chorus 1

Verse 3

$$\begin{array}{ll} \text{G} & \text{D7} \end{array}$$
O Mary, Holiest Mother,

G
As pure as flowers unfolding,

D7
As pure as flowers unfolding.

G
I come on this eve of Christmas,

C
Thy love and glory beholding,

$$\begin{array}{lll} \text{D} & \text{A7} & \text{D} \end{array}$$
Thy love and glory beholding.

Chorus 3

$$\begin{array}{ll} \text{G} & \text{D7} \end{array}$$
Going, going to Bethlehem town,

G
Going, going the Baby to see.

C
To greet His father, Joseph,

$$\begin{array}{lll} \text{A} & \text{D7} & \text{G} \end{array}$$
And Mary, on bended knee.

Good Christian Men, Rejoice

14th Century Latin Text
Translated by John Mason Neale
14th Century German Melody

Melody:

Good Chris - tian men, re - joice,... ____

Verse 1

      G
Good Christian men, rejoice,

With heart and soul and voice;
D7   **G**
Give ye heed to what we say:

       Am7 D7
News! News! Jesus Christ is born today!

       Em
Ox and ass before Him bow,

   Am7 D7   **Em**
And He is in the manger now;
C   **D7**   **G** **D7**
Christ is born to - day!____

G   **D7**   **G**
Christ is born to - day!

Verse 2

      G
Good Christian men, rejoice,

With heart and soul and voice;

D7   **G**
Now ye hear of endless bliss;

      Am7 D7
Joy! Joy! Jesus Christ was born for this!

          Em
He has ope'd the heav'nly door,

     Am7   **D7**   **Em**
And man is blessed evermore.

C   **D7**   **G** **D7**
Christ was born for this!_____

G   **D7**   **G**
Christ was born for this!

Verse 3

      G
Good Christian men, rejoice,

With heart and soul and voice;

D7   **G**
Now ye need not fear the grave;

     Am7 D7
Peace! Peace! Jesus Christ was born to save!

          Em
Calls you and and calls you all,

    Am7   **D7 Em**
To gain His everlasting hall.

C   **D7**   **G** **D7**
Christ was born to save!_____

G   **D7**   **G**
Christ was born to save!

Hark! The Herald Angels Sing

Words by Charles Wesley
Altered by George Whitefield
Music by Felix Mendelssohn-Bartholdy
Arranged by William H. Cummings

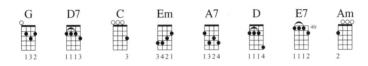

Verse 1

G   D7
Hark! the herald angels sing,

G C D7 G
"Glory to the newborn King!

            Em A7
Peace on earth, and mercy mild,

D   A7 D
God and sinners reconciled!"

G   C D7
Joyful, all ye nations, rise,

G   C D7
Join the triumph of the skies;

C   E7 Am
With th'angelic host proclaim,

D7   G   D7 G
"Christ is born in Bethlehem!"

C   E7   Am
Hark! the herald angels sing,

D7   G   D7   G
"Glory to the newborn King!"

Verse 2

```
G                          D7
Christ, by highest heav'n a - dored,

G         C  D7   G
Christ the everlasting Lord;

                  Em       A7
Late in time be - hold Him come,

D              A7    D
Offspring of the virgin womb.

G                  C       D7
Veiled in flesh, the Godhead see:

G                  C       D7
Hail, th'incarnate Dei - ty;

C         E7        Am
Pleased, as man, with men to dwell,

D7  G     D7     G
Jesus, our Em-man-u -el!

C         E7        Am
Hark! the herald angels sing,

D7    G     D7     G
"Glory to the newborn King!"
```

Verse 3

```
G                              D7
Hail, the heav'n-born Prince of peace!

G     C    D7    G
Hail, the Son of Righteousness!

                  Em    A7
Light and life to all He brings,

D                  A7   D
Ris'n with healing in his wings.

G              C    D7
Mild He lays His glory by,

G              C        D7
Born that man no more may die,

C     E7        Am
Born to raise the sons of earth,

D7    G     D7     G
Born to give them second birth.

C     E7        Am
Hark! the herald angels sing,

D7    G     D7     G
"Glory to the newborn King!"
```

He Is Born

Traditional French Carol

He   is   born,   the __   ho - ly   Child,...

Chorus 1

G
He is born, the holy Child,

                        D
Play the oboe and bagpipes merrily.

G
He is born, the holy Child,

                   D   G
Sing we all of the Savior mild.

<table>
<tr><td>*Verse 1*</td><td>

G   D   G
Through long ages of the past,

               D
Prophets have betold His coming,

G   D   G
Through long ages of the past;

              Am G D7
Now the time has come at last!

</td></tr>
</table>

Verse 1

G　　　　　D　G
Through long ages of the past,

　　　　　　　　D
Prophets have betold His coming,

G　　　　　D　G
Through long ages of the past;

　　　　　　　Am G D7
Now the time has come at last!

Chorus 2

Repeat Chorus 1

Verse 2

G　　　D　G
O how lovely, O how pure

　　　　　　D
Is this perfect Child of heaven;

G　　　D　G
O how lovely, O how pure,

　　　　　Am G D7
Gracious gift of God to man!

Chorus 3

Repeat Chorus 1

Hear Them Bells

Words and Music by
D.S. McCosh

Verse

G
Hear them bells,

D7   G
Merry Christmas bells!

      Am7
They are ringing out the

D7   G
Evil of the sword.

Hear them bells,

D7   G
Merry Christmas bells!

      Am7
They are ringing in the

D7   G
Glory of the Lord!

Hear, O Shepherds

Traditional Croation Carol

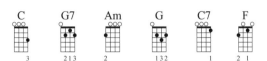

Verse

    C   G7   C
Hear, O shepherds, hear while I tell you,

      G7 C   G7   C
Hark to the miracle that only now befell you:

     Am   G   C   G C7
On a manger lowly, in a prickly stall___

  F   G   Am C   G   C C7
Lies the baby ho - ly___ who will save us all.___

  F   G   Am C   G7   C
Lies the baby ho - ly___ who will save us all.

The Holly and the Ivy

18th Century English Carol

Verse 1

       G   D7 G
The holly and the ivy,

C G   C D
When they are both full grown,

   G   C   D
Of all the trees that are in the wood,

C G   D7 G
The holly bears the crown.

Chorus 1

C G   D7 G
The rising of the sun

C   G   C D
And the running of the deer,

   G   C   D C
The playing of the merry or - gan,

   G   D7 G
Sweet singing in the choir.

Verse 2

   G   D7 G
The holly bears a__ blossom

C G   C D
As white as li - ly flow'r,

   G   C   D
And Mary bore sweet Jesus Christ

C G   D7 G
To be our dear Sav - ior.

Chorus 2   *Repeat Chorus 1*

Verse 3

```
        G        D7  G
The holly bears a__ berry

C G          C D
As red as an - y blood,

        G           C    D
And Mary bore sweet Jesus Christ

C G          D7  G
To do poor sinners good.
```

Chorus 3   *Repeat Chorus 1*

Verse 4

```
        G        D7  G
The holly bears a__ prickle

C G            C D
As sharp as an - y thorn,

        G           C    D
And Mary bore sweet Jesus Christ

C G              D7   G
On Christmas day in the morn.
```

Chorus 4   *Repeat Chorus 1*

Verse 5

```
        G        D7  G
The holly bears a__ bark

C G       C  D
As bitter as the gall,

        G             C    D
And Mary bore sweet Jesus Christ

C  G        D7 G
For to redeem us  all.
```

Chorus 5   *Repeat Chorus 1*

Verse 6   *Repeat Verse 1*

Chorus 6   *Repeat Chorus 1*

How Brightly Beams the Morning Star

Words and Music by Philipp Nicolai
Translated by William Mercer
Harmonized by J.S. Bach

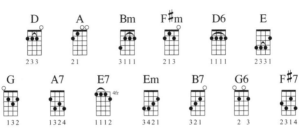

Verse 1

D   A   D Bm   F♯m D6   E   A
How brightly beams the__ morning star!

D   G   A7 D   E7 A   D6   E7 A
What sud-den rad - i - ance from a - far

D   G   D Em D A7   D
Doth glad us with its shin - ing?

A   D Bm F♯m   D6   E   A
The ray of God that__ breaks our night

D   G   A7 D   E7 A   D6   E7   A
And fills the dark - ened souls with light,

D   G   D Em D   A7   D
Who long for truth were pin - ing.

A   D   A   Bm Em D A7   D
Thy word, Je - sus, tru - ly feeds us,

A7   D A   B7
Rightly leads us,

Em Bm   G6 A7   D
Life be - stow - ing.

Bm   F♯7   G   D   G   D G6 A7 D
Praise, oh__ praise such love o'erflow - ing.

Verse 2

D   A   D Bm F#m D6   E A
Through Thee a - lone can we__ be blest;

D   G   A7 D E7 A D6   E7 A
Then deep be on__ our hearts im-prest

D G D Em D A7   D
The love that Thou hast borne us;

A   D Bm F#m D6 E   A
So make us read - y___ to ful - fill

D   G   A7 D E7   A   D6 E7 A
With burning seal___ Thy ho - ly will,

D   G   D Em D A7   D
Though men may vex or scorn us;

A D A Bm Em   D A7 D
Savior, let us__ nev - er lose Thee,

A7 D A   B7
For we choose Thee,

Em Bm G6 A7 D
Thirst to__ know__ Thee,

Bm F#7 G D   G   D G6 A7 D
All are__ we and have we owe__ Thee!

Verse 3

A   D Bm F#m D6 E A
O praise to Him who came to save,

D G A7   D E7 A D6   E7 A
Who conquer'd death and burst the grave;

D G D Em D A7 D
Each day new praise re - soundeth

A   D Bm F#m D6 E   A
To Him the Lamb who once was slain,

D G   A7 D E7   A   D6 E7 A
The Friend who none__ shall trust in vain,

D   G   D Em D A7 D
Whose grace for ay__ a - boundeth;

A   D A Bm Em D A7 D
Sing, ye heavens, tell the sto - ry

A7 D A   B7
Of His glo - ry,

Em Bm   G6 A7 D
Till His__ prais - es

Bm F#m G D   G   D G6 A7 D
Flood with light earth's darkest plac - es!

I Go to Bethlehem

Traditional Czech Carol

Verse 1

   D   **A7**
I go to Bethlehem,

   D   **A7**
To see the tiny child;

   D   **A7**
My black rooster, trim and sleek,

Bm7   **A**
My cuckoo with song so sweet:

   D   **A7** **D**
These will I give Him.

Verse 2

D   A7
Rooster will crow away

D   A7
Making the Baby gay;

D   A7
Cuckoo perching near His little head,

Bm7   A
Calling, softly will make His heart glad:

D   A7 D
These will I give Him.

Outro

D
Coo, coo-coo!

Coo, coo-coo!

A7 D   A7 D
Jesus, He sings for you!

Coo, coo-coo!

Coo, coo-coo!

A7 D   A7 D
Jesus, He sings for you!

I Heard the Bells on Christmas Day

Words by Henry Wadsworth Longfellow
Music by John Baptiste Calkin

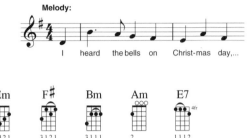

Verse 1

        G   C   D7
I heard the bells on Christmas day,

        Em   F♯   Bm
Their old familiar carols play,

        Am   D7   Bm   E7
And mild and sweet the words re-peat,

        Am   E7   Em   D7
Of peace on earth, goodwill to men.

Verse 2

        G   C   D7
I thought how as the day had come,

        Em   F♯   Bm
The belfries of all Christendom

        Am   D7   Bm   E7
Had rolled a - long th'un - broken song

        Am   E7   D7   G
Of peace on earth, goodwill to men.

Verse 3

```
         G          C          D7
And in despair I bowed my head:

         Em              F#      Bm
"There is no peace on earth," I said,

         Am    D7        Bm         E7
"For hate is strong, and mocks the song

         Am      E7         Em    D7
Of peace on earth, goodwill to men."
```

Verse 4

```
         G                  C       D7
Then pealed the bells more loud and deep:

         Em              F#      Bm
"God is not dead, nor doth He sleep;

         Am        D7      Bm        E7
The wrong shall fail, the right pre - vail,

         Am      E7       D7    G
With peace on earth, goodwill to men."
```

Verse 5

```
         G          C    D7
Till ringing, singing on its way,

         Em                  F#      Bm
The world revolved from night to day,

         Am    D7       Bm      E7
A voice, a chime, a chant sublime,

         Am      E7       D7    G
Of peace on earth, goodwill to men!
```

I Saw Three Ships

Traditional English Carol

Verse 1

G   D7   G   D7
I saw three ships come sailing in

G   D7
On Christmas day, on Christmas day;

G   D7   G   D7
I saw three ships come sailing in

G   D7 G
On Christmas day in the morning.

Verse 2

G   D7   G   D7
And what was in those ships all three

G   D7
On Christmas day, on Christmas day?

G   D7   G   D7
And what was in those ships all three

G   D7 G
On Christmas day in the morning?

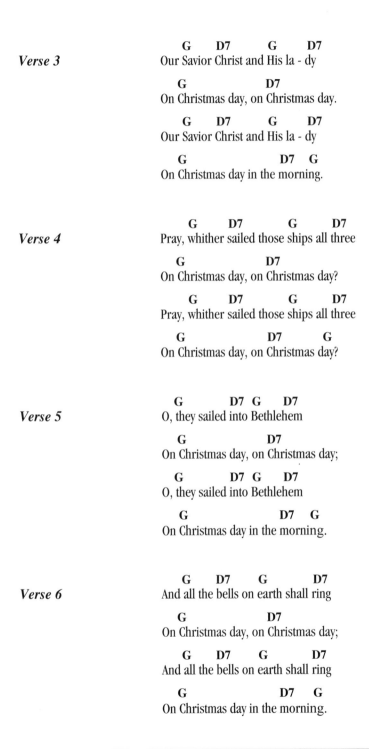

Verse 3

G   D7   G   D7
Our Savior Christ and His la - dy

G   D7
On Christmas day, on Christmas day.

G   D7   G   D7
Our Savior Christ and His la - dy

G   D7 G
On Christmas day in the morning.

Verse 4

G   D7   G   D7
Pray, whither sailed those ships all three

G   D7
On Christmas day, on Christmas day?

G   D7   G   D7
Pray, whither sailed those ships all three

G   D7   G
On Christmas day, on Christmas day?

Verse 5

G   D7 G   D7
O, they sailed into Bethlehem

G   D7
On Christmas day, on Christmas day;

G   D7 G   D7
O, they sailed into Bethlehem

G   D7 G
On Christmas day in the morning.

Verse 6

G   D7   G   D7
And all the bells on earth shall ring

G   D7
On Christmas day, on Christmas day;

G   D7   G   D7
And all the bells on earth shall ring

G   D7 G
On Christmas day in the morning.

Verse 7

G   D7   G   D7
And all the angels in heav'n shall sing

G   D7
On Christmas day, on Christmas day;

G   D7   G   D7
And all the angels in heav'n shall sing

G   D7   G
On Christmas day in the morning.

Verse 8

G   D7   G   D7
And all the souls on earth shall sing

G   D7
On Christmas day, on Christmas day;

G   D7   G   D7
And all the souls on earth shall sing

G   D7   G
On Christmas day in the morning.

Verse 9

G D7 G   D7
Then let us all re - joice a - main

G   D7
On Christmas day, on Christmas day;

G D7 G   D7
Then let us all re - joice a - main

G   D7   G
On Christmas day in the morning!

Infant So Gentle

Traditional French Carol

Verse 1

  E   B7 E   A   E B7 E
Infant so gentle, so pure and so sweet;

        B7 E   A E B7   E
Love from Thy tiny eyes sinners doth greet.

 B7   E A E B7   E
Tend'rest words fail all Thy beauty to show;

       B7 E   A   E A   E B7   E
We must a - dore Thee, if Thee we would know.

Verse 2

  E   B7 E   A   E B7 E
Infant so holy, so meek and so mild,

        B7 E   A E B7   E
We come to welcome Thee, our dear Christ child.

 B7   E   A   E B7   E
We cannot tell Thee how much we do need,

      B7   E   A   E A E   B7 E
Thy precious presence; all sinners take heed.

Infant Holy, Infant Lowly

Traditional Polish Carol
Paraphrased by Edith M.G. Reed

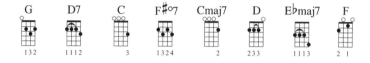

Verse 1

       G   D7
Infant holy, Infant lowly,

       G   D7 G
For His bed a cattle stall.

          D7
Oxen lowing, little knowing

       G   D7   G
Christ the Babe is Lord of all.

      C   F#°7
Swift are winging angels singing,

    Cmaj7   D
Noels ringing, tidings bringing:

      G   D7   G
Christ the Babe is Lord of all.

```
| E♭maj7        | F       | G
```

                                                 G   D7

Verse 2   Flocks are sleeping, shepherds keeping

          G   D7   G
Vigil till the morning new,

                          D7
Saw the glory, heard the story,

          G   D7   G
Tidings of a Gospel true.

            C   F♯°7
Thus re - joicing, free from sorrow,

         Cmaj7   D
Praises voicing greet the morrow:

          G   D7   G
Christ the Babe was born for you.

Irish Carol

Traditional Irish Carol

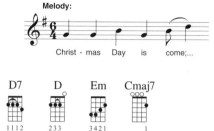

G Em7 C Am D7 D Em Cmaj7

Verse 1

   G   Em7 C G Am
Christmas Day is come; let's all pre - pare for mirth,

D7 G   Em7 C D Em Am G
Which fills the heav'ns and earth at this a - maz - ing birth.

D G   Em7 C   G Am
Through both the joyous angels in strife and hurry fly,

D7 G   Em7   C D Em Am G
With glory and ho - sannas, "All Ho - ly" do they cry,

D7 G   C   D   G   C   D
In_ heav'n the church tri - umphant a - dores with all her choirs,

  Em   Cmaj7 D Em7 C D7 G
The militant on earth with hum - ble faith ad-mires.

Verse 2

   G   Em7   C   G Am
But why should we re - joice? Should we not rather mourn

D7 G   Em7   C D Em Am G
To see the hope of nations thus in a sta - ble born?

D G   Em7   C G   Am
Where are His crown and scepter, where is His throne sub - lime,

D7 G   Em7 C D Em Am G
Where is His throne ma-jestic that should the stars out - shine?

D7 G   C   D   G C D
Is_ there no sumptuous palace, nor any inn at all

  Em   Cmaj7 D Em7 C D7 G
To lodge His heav'nly mother but in_ a_ filth-y stall?

Verse 3

```
        G              Em7       C       G    Am
Oh! Cease, ye blessed angels, such clam'rous joys to make!

D7  G              Em7      C   D   Em Am G
Though midnight silence favors, the shepherds are a - wake;

D   G          Em7     C       G       Am
And you, o glorious star, that with new splendor brings,

D7  G          Em7      C  D  Em   Am G
From the remotest parts three learned east - ern kings,

D7  G        C       D        G       C          D
Turn somewhere else your luster, your rags else - where dis - play,

   Em            Cmaj7   D   Em7 C   D7 G
For Herod may slay the babe, and Christ must straight a - way.
```

Verse 4

```
    G              Em7     C    G    Am
If we would then rejoice, let's cancel the old score,

D7 G        Em7           C   D Em  Am G
And purposing amendment, re - solve to sin_ no_ more;

D   G              Em7      C   G        Am
For mirth can ne'er content us, without a conscience clear;

D7  G              Em7      C D  Em Am G
And thus we'll find true pleasure in all the u - sual cheer,

D7  G      C       D         G       C      D
In__ dancing, sporting, rev'ling, with masquerade and drum,

   Em            Cmaj7 D   Em7 C   D7  G
So Christmas merry  be,_ as Christ - ians doth be - come.
```

It Came Upon the Midnight Clear

Words by Edmund Hamilton Sears
Music by Richard Storrs Willis

Melody:

It came up - on ___ the mid - night clear,...

A   D   B7   E   E7   C#   F#m

Verse 1

```
      A       D      A
It came up - on the midnight clear,

      D      B7    E E7
That glorious song of old,___

      A       D       A
From angels bending near the earth

      D        E       A
To touch their harps of gold:

      C#                    F#m
"Peace on the earth, good-will to men,

      E           B7     E  E7
From heav'n's all-gracious King."___

      A       D       A
The world in solemn stillness lay

      D     E7     A
To hear the angels sing.
```

Verse 2

    A   D   A
Still through the cloven skies they came

    D   B7   E   E7
With peaceful wings un-furled,__

    A   D   A
And still their heavenly music floats

    D   E   A
O'er all the weary world;

   C$\sharp$ F$\sharp$m
A-bove its sad and lowly plains,

    E   B7   E   E7
They bend on hovering wing.__

    A   D   A
And ever o'er its Babel sounds

    D   E7   A
The blessed angels sing.

Verse 3

    A   D   A
And ye, be-neath life's crushing load,

    D   B7   E   E7
Whose forms are bending low,__

    A   D   A
Who toil a-long the climbing way

    D   E   A
With painful steps and slow,

   C$\sharp$ F$\sharp$m
Look now! For glad and golden hours

    E   B7   E   E7
Come swiftly on the wing.__

    A   D   A
O rest be-side the weary road,

    D   E7   A
And hear the angels sing.

Verse 4

    A   D   A
For lo! The days are hastening on,

    D   B7   E   E7
By prophet seen of old,___

     A   D A
When, with the ever-circling years,

     D   E   A
Shall come the time fore-told

     C#   F#m
When peace shall over all the earth

     E   B7   E E7
Its ancient splendors fling,___

     A   D   A
And the whole world send back the song

     D   E7 A
Which now the angels sing.

Jingle Bells

Words and Music by
J. Pierpont

G   C   D7   A7

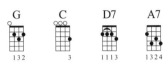

Verse 1

          G
Dashing through the snow,

                      C
In a one-horse open sleigh,

               D7
O'er the fields we go,

            G
Laughing all the way.

Bells on bobtail ring,

          C
Making spirits bright,

            G
What fun it is to ride and sing

  D7   **G**
A sleighing song to-night! Oh!

Chorus 1

G
Jingle bells, jingle bells,

Jingle all the way.

C   G
Oh what fun it is to ride

    A7   D7
In a one-horse open sleigh!

G
Jingle bells, jingle bells,

Jingle all the way.

C   G
Oh what fun it is to ride

    D7   G
In a one-horse open sleigh!

Verse 2

    G
A day or two ago

            C
I thought I'd take a ride,

            D7
And soon Miss Fanny Bright

          G
Was seated by my side.

The horse was lean and lank,

            C
Misfortune seemed his lot,

        G
He got into a drifted bank

    D7   G
And we, we got up-shot! Oh!

Chorus 2   *Repeat Chorus 1*

Verse 3

G
Now the ground is white,

            C
Go it while you're young.

               D7
And take the girls to-night

                 G
And sing this sleighing song.

Just get a bobtail bay,

            C
Two-forty for his speed,

             G
Then hitch him to an open sleigh

    D7   G
And crack, you'll take the lead! Oh!

Chorus 3   *Repeat Chorus 1*

Jolly Old St. Nicholas

Traditional 19th Century American Carol

Melody:

Jol - ly old Saint Nich - o - las,...

G   D#°7   Em   Bm   C   D7

132   1324   3421   3111   2   1112

Verse 1

    G   **D#°7**
Jolly old Saint Nicholas,

Em   **Bm**
Lean your ear this way.

C   **G**
Don't you tell a single soul

D7
What I'm going to say.

G   **D#°7**
Christmas Eve is coming soon,

Em   **Bm**
Now, you dear old man,

C   **G**
Whisper what you'll bring to me;

D7   **G**
Tell me if you can.

Verse 2

G   D#°7
When the clock is striking twelve,

Em   Bm
When I'm fast a-sleep,

C   G
Down the chimney broad and black,

D7
With your pack you'll creep.

G   D#°7
All the stockings you will find

Em   Bm
Hanging in a row.

C   G
Mine will be the shortest one,

D7   G
You'll be sure to know.

Verse 3

G   D#°7
Johnny wants a pair of skates;

Em   Bm
Susy wants a sled;

C   G
Nellie wants a picture book,

D7
Yellow, blue, and red;

G   D#°7
Now I think I'll leave to you

Em   Bm
What to give the rest.

C   G
Choose for me, dear Santa Claus,

D7   G
You will know the best.

Joy to the World

Words by Isaac Watts
Music by George Frideric Handel
Adapted by Lowell Mason

Joy   to   the   world!

D   A7   G

1 1 1 4   1 3 2 4   1 3 2

Verse 1

D   A7 D
Joy to the world! The Lord is_ come;

G A7   D
Let earth re-ceive her King;

Let ev'ry heart prepare Him room,

And heav'n and nature sing,

A7
And heav'n and nature sing,

D   A7 D
And heav'n and heav'n and na-ture sing.

Verse 2

D   A7 D
Joy to the earth! The Sav-ior reigns;

G A7   D
Let men their songs em-ploy;

While fields and floods, rocks, hills and plains

Repeat the sounding joy,

A7
Re-peat the sounding joy,

D   A7 D
Re-peat, repeat the sound-ing joy.

UKULELE CHORD SONGBOOK

Verse 3

   D   A7 D
No more let sin and sor-rows grow,

    G   A7   D
Nor thorns in-fest the ground;

He comes to make His blessings flow

Far as the curse is found,

    A7
Far as the curse is found,

    D   A7 D
Far as, far as the curse is_ found.

Verse 4

   D   A7 D
He rules the world with truth and grace,

    G   A7   D
And makes the nations prove

The glories of His righteousness

And wonders of His love,

    A
And wonders of His love,

    D   A7 D
And wonders, wonders of His love.

Love Came Down at Christmas

Text by Christina Rossetti
Traditional Irish Melody

Melody:

Love came down at Christ - mas,...

G   C   D   Em   Bm   D type2

132 3 122 3421 3111 1114

Verse 1

       G   C D G
Love came down at Christmas,

              C G   D
Love all lovely, love divine;___

Em C   G   C G   D G
Love___ was born at Christmas,___

D G   Bm D type2 Em C G
Star___ and an - gels   gave the sign.

Verse 2

       G   C D G
Worship we the God-head,

           C   G   D
Love incarnate, love divine;___

Em C   G C G   D G
Wor - ship we our Je - sus,___

D G   Bm D type2 Em C   G
But___ wherewith for   sa - cred sign?

Verse 3

       G   C D G
Love shall be our to - ken;

          C G   D
Love be yours and love be mine,___

Em C   G   C G   D G
Love___ to God and neighbor,___

D G   Bm D type2 Em C G
Love___ for plea and   gift and sign.

O Come, Little Children

Words by C. von Schmidt
Music by J.P.A. Schulz

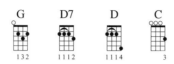

Verse 1

     G   **D7**   **G**
O come, little children, from cot and from hall,

           D7   **G**
O come to the manger in Bethlehem's stall.

  D   **D7** **G**   **C**
There meekly He lieth, the heavenly Child,

  D   **G**   **D7**   **G**
So poor and so humble, so sweet and so mild.

Verse 2

     G   **D7**   **G**
Now "Glory to God" sing the angels on high,

          D7   **G**
And "Peace upon earth" heav'nly voices re-ply.

  D   **D7**   **G**   **C**
Then come, little children, and join in the day

  D   **G**   **D7**   **G**
That gladdened the world on that first Christmas day.

O Christmas Tree

Traditional German Carol

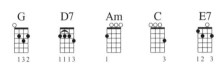

Verse 1

    G   **D7 G**
O Christmas tree, O Christmas tree,

    Am   **D7 G**
You stand in verdant beauty!

        D7 G
O Christmas tree, O Christmas tree,

    Am   **D7 G**
You stand in verdant beauty!

        C   **D7**
Your boughs are green in summer's glow,

        G
And do not fade in winter's snow.

D7 G   **D7 G**   **E7**
O_ Christmas tree, O_ Christmas tree,

    Am   **D7 G**
You stand in verdant beauty!

Verse 2

```
         G              D7 G
O Christmas tree, O  Christmas tree,

        Am         D7  G
Much pleasure doth thou bring me!

                 D7 G
O Christmas tree, O  Christmas tree,

        Am         D7  G
Much pleasure doth thou bring me!

            C      D7
For ev'ry year the Christmas tree

                    G
Brings to us all both joy and glee.

D7 G            D7 G        E7
O_ Christmas tree, O_ Christmas tree,

        Am         D7  G
Much pleasure doth thou bring me!
```

Verse 3

```
         G              D7 G
O Christmas tree, O_ Christmas tree,

        Am         D7 G
Thy candles shine out brightly!

                 D7 G
O Christmas tree, O_ Christmas tree,

        Am         D7 G
Thy candles shine out brightly!

                C      D7
Each bough doth hold its tiny light

                    G
That makes each toy to sparkle bright.

D7 G            D7 G        E7
O_ Christmas tree, O_ Christmas tree,

        Am         D7 G
Thy candles shine out brightly!
```

O Come, All Ye Faithful

(Adeste Fideles)

Words and Music by John Francis Wade
Latin Words translated by Frederick Oakeley

Melody:

O come, all ye faith - ful,...

G	D	C	Em	A7	D type2

132   122   3   3421   1324   1114

Verse 1

      G   **D**   **G**   **C**   **G D**
O come all ye faithful, joyful and tri-um-phant,

      Em   **A7** **D type2 G**
O come ye, o come ye to

D type2 A7   **D type2**
Beth - le - hem.

G   **D**   **C**   **G**   **D**   **Em**   **D type2**
Come and behold Him, born the King of angels.

Chorus 1

      G   **D** **G**
O come let us a-dore Him,

         D **G**   **D**
O come let us a-dore Him,

     C   **A7** **D type2 C**
O come let us a-dore Him,

G **D**   **G**
Christ__ the Lord.

Verse 2

     G   D   G   C   G D
Sing choirs of angels, sing in ex - ul - ta - tion,

     Em A7 D^{type2} G
Sing, all_ ye citizens of

D^{type2} A7 D^{type2}
heav - en a - bove.

   G D   C G D   Em D^{type2}
Glo-ry to God__ in the high - est.

Chorus 2   *Repeat Chorus 1*

Verse 3

     G   D   G   C   G D
Yea, Lord, we greet Thee, born this happy morning.

     Em A7 D^{type2}G
Je-sus, to Thee be   all

     D^{type2}A7 D^{type2}
glo-ry_____ giv'n.

   G   D   C G D   Em D^{type2}
Word of the Father, now in flesh ap-pearing.

Chorus 3   *Repeat Chorus 1*

O Come, O Come Emmanuel

Plainsong, 13th Century
Words translated by John M. Neale
and Henry S. Coffin

Em   Am   D   G   C   Bm   A7   D^{type2}

Verse 1

         Em   Am D   G
O come, O come, Em - man - u - el,

         Em   C   Am Bm Em
And ransom captive Is - ra - el,

         Am   Em A7 D^{type2}
That mourns in lonely ex - ile here

         Em   Am D   G
Un-til the Son of God__ ap-pear.

Chorus 1

         D^{type2}   Em
Re-joice, re-joice!

         C D^{type2} Em   G   C   Am Bm Em
Em - man - u - el shall come to Thee, O Is - ra - el!

Verse 2

         Em   Am D   G
O come, Thou Dayspring, come__and cheer

         Em   C   Am Bm   Em
Our spirits by Thine ad - vent here;

         Am   Em A7   D^{type2}
Dis-perse the gloomy clouds__ of night,

         Em   Am D   G
And death's dark shadows put___ to flight.

Chorus 2   *Repeat Chorus 1*

Verse 3

```
        Em              Am  D    G
O come, Thou Wisdom, from__ on high,

        Em   C       Am  Bm   Em
And order all things far____ and nigh;

        Am          Em  A7     D type2
To us the path of know - ledge show,

        Em          Am  D    G
And cause us in her ways__ to go.
```

Chorus 3   *Repeat Chorus 1*

Verse 4

```
        Em          Am  D    G
O come, desire of na - tions, bind

      Em   C    Am  Bm    Em
All people in one heart__ and mind;

        Am          Em  A7    D type2
Bid envy, strife, and quar - rels cease;

      Em                Am  D    G
Fill the whole world with heav - en's peace.
```

Chorus 4   *Repeat Chorus 1*

Verse 5

```
        Em            Am  D   G
O come, Thou Key of Da - vid, come,

      Em   C       Am  Bm   Em
And open wide our heav - 'nly home.

        Am            Em  A7   D type2
Make safe the way that leads__ on high,

      Em            Am  D    G
And close the path to mis - er - y.
```

Chorus 5   *Repeat Chorus 1*

O Holy Night

French Words by Placide Cappeau
English Words by John S. Dwight
Music by Adolphe Adam

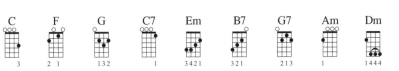

Verse 1

      C   F   C
O holy night, the stars are brightly shining,

                  G   C
It is the night of the dear Savior's birth;

                     F   C C7
Long lay the world in sin and error pin - ing,

            Em   B7   Em
Till He ap-peared and the soul felt its worth.

  G7   C
A thrill of hope, the weary world rejoices,

  G7   C
For yonder breaks a new and glorious morn;

Am   Em   Dm   Am
Fall on your knees! O, hear the angel voices!

  C G7   C F   C G7   C
O night__ di-vine,__ O night__ when Christ was born!

  G G7   C F C   G7   C
O night,__ O ho - ly night, O night di-vine!

Verse 2

C   F   C
Truly He taught us to love one an-other,

                                 G   C
His law is love, and His gospel is peace;

                                    F   C   C7
Chains shall He break, for the slave is our broth-er,

             Em   B7   Em
And in His name all op-pression shall cease.

        G7   C
Sweet hymns of joy in grateful chorus raise we,

        G7   C
Let all within us praise His holy name;

Am   Em   Dm   Am
Christ is the Lord, O praise His name for-ever!

   C G7   C   F   C G7   C
His pow'r__ and glo - ry ev - er more pro-claim!

   G G7   C   F   C G7   C
His pow'r__ and glo - ry ev - er more pro-claim!

O Little Town of Bethlehem

Words by Phillips Brooks
Music by Lewis H. Redner

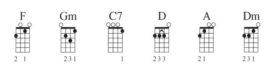

Verse 1

      F   **Gm**
O little town of Bethlehem,

      C7   **F**
How still we see thee lie!

        D   **Gm**
Above thy deep and dreamless sleep

     C7   **F**
The silent stars go by.

     C7   **A**
Yet in thy dark streets shineth

   Dm   **A**
The everlasting light.

     F   **Gm**
The hopes and fears of all the years

     C7   **F**
Are met in thee to-night.

Verse 2

    F   Gm
For Christ is born of Mary,

   C7   F
And gathered all a-bove,

      D   Gm
While mortals sleep, the angels keep

   C7   F
Their watch of wond'ring love.

    C7   A
O morning stars, to-gether

   Dm   A
Pro-claim the holy birth!

    F   Gm
And praises sing to God the King,

   C7   F
And peace to men on earth!

Verse 3

    F   Gm
How silently, how silently

   C7   F
The wondrous gift is giv'n!

     D   Gm
So God im-parts to human hearts

   C7   F
The blessings of His heav'n.

    C7   A
No ear may hear His coming,

   Dm   A
But in this world of sin,

    F   Gm
Where meek souls will re-ceive Him still,

   C7   F
The dear Christ enters in.

Verse 4

       F   **Gm**
O holy Child of Bethlehem,

      C7   **F**
De-scend to us, we pray;

        D   **Gm**
Cast out our sin and enter in;

    C7   **F**
Be born in us to-day.

        C7   **A**
We hear the Christmas angels

   Dm   **A**
The great glad tidings tell;

   F   **Gm**
O come to us, a-bide with us,

    C7   **F**
Our Lord Em-man-u-el!

Rejoice and Be Merry

Traditional English

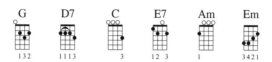

G   D7   C   E7   Am   Em

Verse

      G   **D7**   **G**   **D7**
Re-joice and be merry in songs and in mirth!

G C   **G**   **C D7 G**
O praise our Re-deemer, all mor - tals on earth!

           D7   **E7**   **Am**
For this is the birthday of Jesus our King,

D7 Em   **D7**   **G C D7 G**
Who brought us sal-vation His prais - es we'll sing!

Once in Royal David's City

Words by Cecil F. Alexander
Music by Henry J. Gauntlett

Melody:

Once in roy - al Da - vid's _ cit - y...

G   Bm   D7   C

132   3111   1112   3

Verse 1

G
Once in royal David's city

Bm D7 G
Stood a lowly cattle shed,

Where a mother laid her Baby

Bm   D7   G
In a manger for His bed.

C   G   D7   G
Mary was that mother mild,

C   G   D7 G
Jesus Christ her little Child.

Verse 2

G
He came down to earth from heaven,

Bm   D7   G
Who is God and Lord of all,

And His shelter was a stable,

Bm   D7   G
And His cradle was a stall.

C   G   D7   G
With the poor, and mean, and lowly,

C   G   D7   G
Lived on earth our Savior holy.

Verse 3

G
Jesus is our childhood's pattern,

    Bm   D7 G
Day by day like us He grew;

He was little, weak and helpless,

       Bm   D7   G
Tears and smiles like us He knew.

C   G   D7   G
And He feeleth for our sadness,

C   G   D7   G
And He shareth in our gladness.

Verse 4

G
And our eyes at last shall see Him,

      Bm   D7   G
Through His own re-deeming love,

For that child so dear and gentle

    Bm   D7   G
Is our Lord in heav'n a-bove.

C   G   D7   G
And He leads His children on

C   G   D7 G
To the place where He is gone.

Pat-A-Pan

(Willie, Take Your Little Drum)

Words and Music by
Bernard de la Monnoye

Wil - lie, take your lit - tle drum,...

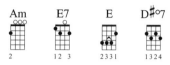

Verse 1

       Am   **E7** **Am**
Willie, take your little drum,

      E7   **E**   **D#°7** **E**
Robin, bring your whis - tle,__ come.

                Am
When we hear the fife and drum,

                   E
Tu-re-lu-re-lu, pat-a-pat-a-pan.

                Am
When we hear the fife and drum,

      E7   **Am E** **Am**
Christmas should be light and fun.

Verse 2

        Am   E7   Am
Thus the men of olden days

        E7   E   D♯°7 E
Gave the King of Kings their praise.

               Am
When they hear the fife and drum,

               E
Tu-re-lu-re-lu, pat-a-pat-a-pan.

               Am
With the drums they sing and play,

        E7   Am   E   Am
Full of joy on Christ-mas day.

Verse 3

        Am   E7   Am
God and man are now be-come

        E7   E D♯°7 E
Closely joined as fife and__ drum.

               Am
When we play the fife and drum,

               E
Tu-re-lu-re-lu, pat-a-pat-a-pan.

               Am
When on fife and drum we play,

        E7   Am E Am
Dance and make the hol - i - day.

Ring Out, Ye Wild and Merry Bells

Words and Music by
C. Maitland

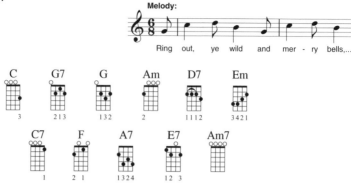

Verse 1

      C   **G7**   **C**   **G7**
Ring out, ye wild and merry bells,

      C   **G7** **C**
Ring out the old, old sto - ry

         G7   **C**   **G7**
That first was told by angel tongues

      G   **Am**   **D7** **G**
From out the realms of glo - ry.

Em
Peace on earth was their sweet song,

       D7 **G7**
Glory in the high-est!

C7   **F** **A7 D7 G7**
Echoing all the hills away,

E7   **Am7 D7 G7** **C**
Glory in___ the high-est!

Chorus 1

    F   C7 F
Ring, sweet bells, ring ever-more,

                     C7   F
Peal from ev'ry stee - ple.

    D7   G7   E7   Am
Christ, the Lord, shall be our God

          C   Am G7   C
And we shall be His peo - ple!

Verse 2

        C   G7   C   G7
Ring out, ye silv'ry bells, ring out,

       C   G7 C
Ring out your exul-ta - tion

            G7   C   G7
That God with man is recon-ciled.

       Am   D7 G
Go tell it to the na - tions.

    Em
Therefore let us all today,

             D7 G7
Glory in the high-est!

    C7   F   A7 D7   G7
Banish sor - row far a-way,

    E7   Am7 D7 G7   C
Glory in__ the high - est!

Chorus 2   *Repeat Chorus 1*

Rise Up, Shepherd, and Follow

African-American Spiritual

Melody:

There's a star in the east on Christ-mas morn,...

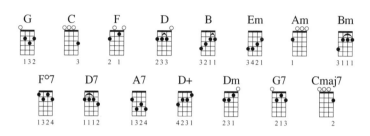

G	C	F	D	B	Em	Am	Bm
132	3	2 1	233	3211	3421	1	3111

F°7	D7	A7	D+	Dm	G7	Cmaj7
1324	1112	1324	4231	231	213	2

Verse 1

        G
There's a star in the east on Christmas morn,

C   **F**   **D**
Rise up, shepherd, and follow.

       G   **B**
It will lead to the place where the Savior's born,

Em   **Am**   **G**
Rise up, shepherd, and follow.

Chorus 1

Em   Bm   C   G
Leave your ewes and leave your lambs,

D   F°7   D7
Rise up, shepherd, and follow.

Em   Bm   C   G
Leave your sheep and leave your rams,

A7   Am   G
Rise up, shepherd, and follow.

D+ D7
Follow, fol - low,

Dm   D+
Rise up, shepherd, and follow.

G   G7   Cmaj7
Follow the star of Beth-le-hem,___

A7   Am   G D
Rise up, shepherd, and fol - low.

Verse 2

G
If you take good heed to the angel's word,

C   F   D
Rise up, shepherd, and follow.

G   B
You'll for-get all your flocks, you'll forget your herd,

Em   Am   G
Rise up, shepherd, and follow.

Verse 2   *Repeat Chorus 1*

Rocking

Traditional Czech Carol

Melody:

Ba - by Je - sus, gen - tly __ sleep,...

G   A7   D   A   C   Am

Verse 1

      G   A7 D   A   D
Baby Jesus, gently sleep, do not stir;

    C   G   D   G
We will bring a coat of fur.

            C   D
We will rock you, rock you, rock you,

    G   C   Am D
Gently slumber as we rock you,

    G   A7   D
See the fur to keep you warm,

    C   G   D G
Snugly fits your tiny form.

Verse 2

      G   A7 D   A   D
Mary's precious baby sleep, gently sleep,

    C   G   D   G
Sleep in comfort, slumber deep.

            C   D
We will rock you, rock you, rock you,

    G   C   Am D
Gently slumber as we rock you,

    G   A7   D
We will praise you all we can,

    C   G   D G
Darling, darling little man.

The Sleep of the Infant Jesus

Traditional French Carol

Melody:

Here, 'mid the ass and ox - en mild,...

Em   B   B7   G   C   D   Am

Verse 1

```
Em                    B    Em B7
Here, 'mid the ass and ox - en  mild,

Em   G    C             B
Sleep, sleep, sleep, thou tiny Child.

Em           D    G          C
Thousand cheru-bim, thousand sera-phim,

             Em           Am  B7 Em
Guarding o'er the bed of the great Lord of love.
```

Verse 2

```
Em                    B    Em B7
Here, 'mid the rose and lil - y  bright,

Em   G    C             B
Sleep, sleep, sleep, thou tiny Child.

Em                 B   Em  B7
Here, 'mid the shepherds' glad de - light,

Em   G    C             B
Sleep, sleep, sleep, thou tiny Child.

Em           D    G          C
Thousand cheru-bim, thousand sera-phim,

             Em           Am B7 Em
Guarding o'er the bed of the great Lord of  love.
```

Silent Night

Words by Joseph Mohr
Translated by John F. Young
Music by Franz X. Gruber

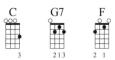

Verse 1

C
Silent night, holy night!

G7 C
All is calm, all is bright.

F   C
Round yon Virgin Mother and Child.

F   C
Holy Infant so tender and mild,

G7   C
Sleep in heavenly peace,

    G7 C
Sleep in heavenly peace.

Verse 2

C
Silent night, holy night!

G7   C
Shepherds quake at the sight.

F   C
Glories stream from heaven afar,

F   C
Heavenly hosts sing Alleluia,

G7   C
Christ the Savior is born!

     G7   C
Christ the Savior is born.

Verse 3

C
Silent night, holy night!

G7   C
Son of God, love's pure light.

F   C
Radiant beams from Thy holy face

F   C
With the dawn of re-deeming grace,

G7   C
Jesus Lord at Thy birth.

     G7   C
Jesus Lord at Thy birth.

The Snow Lay on the Ground

Traditional Irish Carol

The snow lay on the ground,...

Verse 1

    G   **D7 G   D**
The snow lay on the ground, the star shone bright,

                     D7 G   D7 G
When Christ our Lord was born on Christmas night.

            D7 G   D
Venite adoremus Do-mi-num;

            D7 G D G
Venite adoremus Do-mi-num.

Chorus 1

    G   **Am E Am**
Venite adoremus Do-mi-num;

       D7   G D7 G
Venite adoremus Do-mi-num.

Verse 2

     G   **D7 G D**
'Twas Mary, Virgin pure, of ho - ly Anne,

       D7 G D7 G
That brought into this world the God made man.

      D7 G D
She laid Him in a stall at Beth-le-hem,

      D7 G D G
The ass and oxen share the night with them.

Chorus 2   *Repeat Chorus 1*

Verse 3

     G   **D7 G D**
Saint Joseph, too, was by to tend the Child;

      D7 G D7 G
To guard Him and protect His Moth-er mild;

      D7 G D
The Angels hovered round and sang this song:

     D7 G D7 G
Venite adoremus Do-mi-num.

Chorus 3   *Repeat Chorus 1*

Star of the East

Words by George Cooper
Music by Amanda Kennedy

Star of the East, oh, Beth - le - hem's star,...

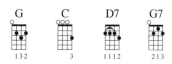

G   C   D7   G7

Verse 1

        G   **C**   **G**
Star of the East, oh, Bethlehem's star,

                     D7
Guiding us on to heaven a-far!

        G   **C**   **G**
Sorrow and grief are lull'd by thy light,

          D7   **G**   **D7**   **G**
Thou hope of each mortal in death's lonely night!

        C   **G**
Fearless and tranquil, we look up to thee,

        D7   **G** **G7**
Knowing thou beam'st thro' e-ter-ni-ty!

        C   **G**
Help us to follow where thou still dost guide,

        D7   **G**
Pilgrims of earth so wide.

UKULELE CHORD SONGBOOK

Verse 2

G   C   G
Star of the East, thou hope of the soul,

                                              D7
While round us here the dark billows roll.

G   C   G
Lead us from sin to glory a-far,

      D7   G   D7   G
Thou star of the East, thou sweet Bethl'em's star.

          D7   G C G
Oh star that leads to God a - bove,

      D7   G   D7
Whose rays are peace and joy and love.

      G   D7   G C G
Watch o'er us still 'til life hath ceased.

      D7   G   D7   G
Beam on, bright star, sweet Bethlehem star!

Still, Still, Still

Salzburg Melody, c.1819
Traditional Austrian Text

Melody:

Still, ___ still, ___ still,...

D   Bm   Em   A7   A

Verse 1

  D **Bm**
Still, still, still,

  Em **A7** **D**
To sleep is now His will.

 A   **D**
On Mary's breast He rests in slumber

A   **D**
While we pray in endless number.

  Bm
Still, still, still,

  Em **A** **D**
To sleep is now His will.

Verse 2

  D **Bm**
Sleep, sleep, sleep,

  Em **A7 D**
While we Thy vigil keep.

  A   **D**
And angels come from heaven singing

A **D**
Songs of jubi-lation bringing

  Bm
Sleep, sleep, sleep,

  Em **A** **D**
While we Thy vigil keep.

  Bm
Sleep, sleep, sleep,

  Em **A** **D**
While we Thy vigil keep.

Wexford Carol

Traditional Irish Carol

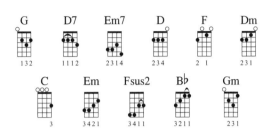

Verse 1

      G   **D7**   **G**
Good people all,__ this Christmas time,

    D7   **Em7 D**   **F**   **Dm D**
Con-sider well__ and bear in mind,__

      G   **D7**   **G**
What our good God__ for us has done

    C   **Em D**   **C**   **G**
In sending His____ be-loved Son.

      Fsus2 F **B♭**
With Mary holy we should pray

   Gm   **C**   **Dm**   **D**
To God with love__ this Christmas day;__

   G   **D7**   **G**
In Bethlehem__ up-on that morn

      C   **Em** **D**   **C** **G**
There was a blessed__ Mes-siah born.

```
               G               D7      G
Verse 2        The night before__ that happy tide
                 D7     Em7 D    F        Dm  D
               The noble Vir  -  gin and her guide__
                  G                D7      G
               Were long time seek  -  ing up and down
                C      Em D      C      G
               To find a lodg  -  ing in the town.
                 Fsus2      F          B♭
               But mark how all things came to pass:
                  Gm         C       Dm         D
               From ev'ry door__ re - pelled, alas!__
                G              D7       G
               As long foretold,__ their refuge all
                 C     Em  D      C   G
               Was but a hum  -  ble ox's stall.


                G            D7      G
Verse 3        Near Bethlehem__ did shepherds keep
                  D7        Em7  D       F        Dm   D
               Their flocks of lambs__ and feeding sheep;__
                G                D7      G
               To whom God's an  -  gels did appear,
                   C      Em  D         C        G
               Which put the shep  -  herds in great fear.
                  Fsus2     F         B♭
               "Pre-pare and go," the angels said,
                 Gm         C      Dm        D
               "To Bethlehem,__ be not afraid;___
                 G               D7       G
               For there you'll find,__ this happy morn,
                C         Em  D          C    G
               A princely babe,__ sweet Jesus born."
```

Verse 4

      G   D7   G
With thankful heart__ and joyful mind,

     D7   Em7 D   F   Dm D
The shepherds went__ the Babe to find,___

      G   D7   G
And as God's an - gel had foretold,

      C   Em D   C   G
They did our Sav - ior Christ be-hold.

     Fsus2 F   B♭
With-in a__ manger He was laid,

     Gm   C   Dm   D
And by His side__ the Virgin maid,___

     G   D7   G
At-tending on__ the Lord of life,

      C   Em D   C   G
Who came on earth__ to end all strife.

Verse 5

      G   D7   G
There were three wise___ men from afar

 D7   Em7 D F   Dm D
Di-rected by___ a glorious star,___

      G   D7   G
And on they wan - dered night and day

      C   Em D   C   G
Un-til they came__ where Jesus lay,

     Fsus2   F   B♭
And when they came un-to that place

       Gm   C   Dm   D
Where our beloved__ Mes-siah was,___

      G   D7   G
They humbly cast__ them at His feet,

      C   Em D   C   G
With gifts of gold___ and incense sweet.

There's a Song in the Air

Words and Music by Josiah G. Holland
and Karl P. Harrington

A 　E7 　E 　B7 　A7 　D 　Dm

Verse 1

      A   E7   A   E7
There's a song in the air! There's a star in the sky!

      A   E   B7   E
There's a mother's deep prayer and a baby's low cry!

      A   E7
And the star rains its fire while the beautiful sing,

      A7   D   Dm E7   A
For the manger of Bethle-hem cradles a King!

Verse 2

      A   E7   A   E7
There's a tumult of joy o'er the wonderful birth,

      A   E   B7   E
For the virgin's sweet boy is the Lord of the earth.

      A   E7
Ay! The star rains its fire while the beautiful sing,

      A7   D   Dm E7   A
For the manger of Bethle-hem cradles a King!

Verse 3

A   E7   A   E7
In the light of that star lie the ages im-pearled;

A   E   B7   E
And that song from a-far has swept over the world.

A   E7
Ev'ry hearth is aflame, and the beautiful sing

A7   D   Dm E7   A
In the homes of the nations that Jesus is King!

Verse 4

A   E7   A   E7
We re-joice in the light, and we echo the song

A   E   B7   E
That comes down through the night from the heavenly throng.

A   E7
Ay! We shout to the lovely e-vangel they bring,

A7   D   Dm E7   A
And we greet in His cradle our Savior and King!

To Us Is Born a Little Child

Traditional German Carol

Melody:

To us is born ___ a...

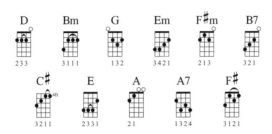

Verse 1

D   Bm GD   G   D
To us is born a lit - tle Child

Bm   G   Em D   F#m   B7 C#
Of_ Ma-ry, maiden Moth - er mild,

E   A   DG   A D   A7 F#
Yule-time a mer-ry sea - son is,

A   D   A   G   A7   D
Babe Jesus our de - light and bliss.

Chorus 1

D   A7   G   A7   D D7 G
O Je - sus dar - ling of my heart,

D   A   G   A7   D
How rich in mercy, Babe, Thou art.

Verse 2

```
D              Bm GD   G D
Strange sight with-in___ a sta - ble old,

Bm  G  EmD      F#m B7  C#
Lo,_ God is_born in want and cold,

E A   D  G    A  D   A7F#
O self - ish world this Babe, I_ say,

A   D     A   G   A7 D
Doth put thee to the blush to - day.
```

Chorus 2   *Repeat Chorus 1*

Verse 3

```
D              Bm G D   G D
Now angels' joy - ful hymns up-raise,

Bm  G   Em D      F#m B7 C#
And God's own Son with car - ols praise.

E  A   D G  A D  A7   F#
To Beth-le-hem the shep-herds fare,

A   D    A   G   A7 D
And firstlings of their flock they bear.
```

Chorus 3   *Repeat Chorus 1*

'Twas the Night Before Christmas

Words by Clement Clark Moore
Music by F. Henri Klickman

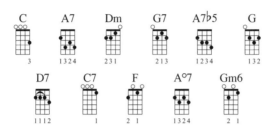

Verse 1

       C   **A7**   **Dm**   **G7**
'Twas the night before Christmas, when all through the house,

 Dm   **G7**   **C**
Not a creature was stirring, not even a mouse.

                  A7♭5   **G**
The stockings were hung by the chimney with care,

      D7   **G7**
In the hopes that Saint Nicholas soon would be there.

    C   **A7**   **Dm**   **G7**
The children were nestled all snug in their beds,

 Dm **G7**   **C**   **C7**
While visions of sugar plums danced through their heads.

 F   **A°7**   **C** **Gm6 A7**
And mamma in her 'kerchief, and I__ in my cap,

   D7   **G7**   **C**
Had just settled our brains for a long winter's nap.

Verse 2

     C   A7   Dm   G
When out on the lawn there a-rose such a clatter,

Dm   G7   C
I sprang from the bed to see what was the matter.

                A7b5   G
Away to the window I flew like a flash,

      D7   G7
Tore open the shutters and threw up the sash.

     C   A7   Dm   G7
The moon on the breast of the new-fallen snow

     Dm   G7   C   C7
Gave a lustre of midday to objects be-low.

    F   A°7   C Gm6   A7
When, what to my wondering eyes should ap - pear,

     D7   G7   C
But a miniature sleigh and eight tiny rein - deer,

Verse 3

     C   A7   Dm   G7
With a little old driver, so lively and quick,

Dm   G7   C
I knew in a moment it must be St. Nick.

              A7b5   G
More rapid than eagles his coursers they came,

     D7   G7
And he whistled, and shouted, and called them by name:

     C   A7   Dm   G7
"Now, Dasher! Now, Dancer! Now, Prancer and Vixen!

    Dm   G7   C   C7
On, Comet! On Cupid! On, Donner and Blitzen!

    F   A°7   C Gm6 A7
To the top of the porch, to the top of the wall!

     D7   G7   C
Now dash away! Dash away! Dash away all!"

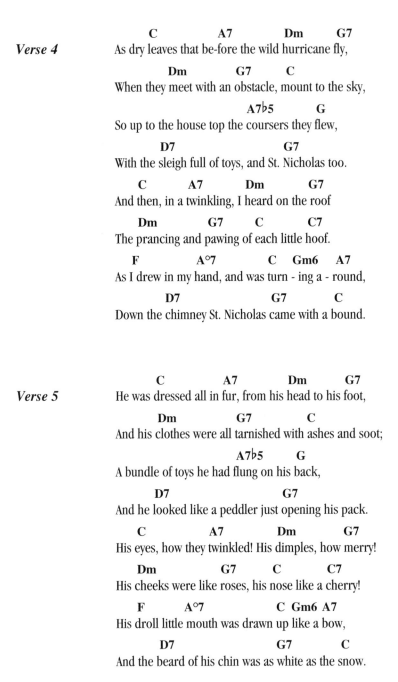

Verse 4

      C   A7   Dm   G7
As dry leaves that be-fore the wild hurricane fly,

      Dm   G7   C
When they meet with an obstacle, mount to the sky,

           A7♭5   G
So up to the house top the coursers they flew,

      D7   G7
With the sleigh full of toys, and St. Nicholas too.

      C   A7   Dm   G7
And then, in a twinkling, I heard on the roof

    Dm   G7   C   C7
The prancing and pawing of each little hoof.

   F   A°7   C Gm6 A7
As I drew in my hand, and was turn - ing a - round,

    D7   G7   C
Down the chimney St. Nicholas came with a bound.

Verse 5

      C   A7   Dm   G7
He was dressed all in fur, from his head to his foot,

    Dm   G7   C
And his clothes were all tarnished with ashes and soot;

        A7♭5   G
A bundle of toys he had flung on his back,

    D7   G7
And he looked like a peddler just opening his pack.

    C   A7   Dm   G7
His eyes, how they twinkled! His dimples, how merry!

   Dm   G7   C   C7
His cheeks were like roses, his nose like a cherry!

   F   A°7   C Gm6 A7
His droll little mouth was drawn up like a bow,

    D7   G7   C
And the beard of his chin was as white as the snow.

Verse 6

       C   A7   Dm   G7
The stump of a pipe he held tight in his teeth,

     Dm   G7   C
And the smoke, it en - circled his head like a wreath.

                 A7♭5   G
He had a broad face and a little round belly

   D7   G7
That shook, when he laughed, like a bowl full of jelly.

       C   A7   Dm   G7
He was chubby and plump, a right jolly old elf,

     Dm   G7   C   C7
And I laughed when I saw him, in spite of my-self;

   F   A°7   C Gm6 A7
A wink of his eye, and a twist of his head,

   D7   G7   C
Soon gave me to know I had nothing to dread.

Verse 7

       C   A7   Dm   G7
He spoke not a word, but went straight to his work,

     Dm   G7   C
And filled all the stockings; then turned with a jerk,

              A7♭5   G
And laying his finger a - side of his nose,

   D7   G7
And giving a nod, up the chimney he rose.

       C   A7   Dm   G7
He sprang to his sleigh, to his team gave a whistle,

     Dm   G7   C   C7
And a-way they all fled like the down of a thistle.

   F   A°7   C Gm6 A7
But I heard him ex - claim, ere he drove out of sight,

   D7   G7   C
"Happy Christmas to all, and to all a good night!"

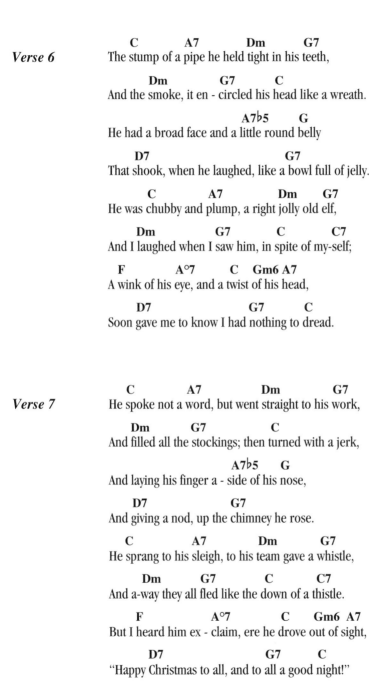

The Twelve Days of Christmas

Traditional English Carol

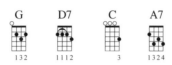

G   D7   C   A7

Verse 1

                   G   D7   G
On the first day of Christmas, my true love sent to me

                            D7   G C G
A partridge in a pear tree._____

Verse 2

                   G   D7   G
On the second day of Christmas, my true love sent to me

D7
Two turtle doves

                   G   D7   G C G
And a partridge in a pear tree.___

Verse 3

                   G   D7   G
On the third day of Christmas, my true love sent to me

D7
Three French hens...
Etc., counting back to "A partridge in a pear tree"

Verse 4

                   G   D7   G
On the fourth day of Christmas, my true love sent to me

D7
Four calling birds...

Verse 5

              G   **D7**   **G**
On the fifth day of Christmas, my true love sent to me

    A7   **D7**
Five golden rings...

Verse 6

              G   **D7**   **G**
On the sixth day of Christmas, my true love gave to me

D7
Six geese a-laying...

Verse 7

              G   **D7**   **G**
On the seventh day of Christmas, my true love gave to me

D7
Seven swans a-swimming...

Verse 8

              G   **D7**   **G**
On the eighth day of Christmas, my true love gave to me

D7
Eight maids a-milking...

Verse 9

              G   **D7**   **G**
On the ninth day of Christmas, my true love gave to me

D7
Nine ladies dancing...

Verse 10

              G   **D7**   **G**
On the tenth day of Christmas, my true love gave to me

D7
Ten lords a-leaping...

Verse 11

              G   **D7**   **G**
On the eleventh day of Christmas, my true love gave to me

D7
Eleven pipers piping...

Verse 12

              G   **D7**   **G**
On the twelfth day of Christmas, my true love gave to me

D7
Twelve drummers drumming...

Up on the Housetop

Words and Music by
B.R. Handy

Verse 1

G
Up on the housetop reindeer pause,

C   **G**   **D7**
Out jumps good old Santa Claus;

G
Down through the chimney with lots of toys,

C   **G**   **D7**   **G**
All for the little ones, Christmas joys.

Chorus 1

C   **G**
Ho, ho, ho! Who wouldn't go?

D7   **G**
Ho, ho, ho! Who wouldn't go?

                         C   **G**   **C**
Up on the housetop, click, click, click,

G   **D7**   **G**
Down through the chimney with good Saint Nick.

Verse 2

G
First comes the stocking of little Nell;

C   G   D7
Oh, dear Santa, fill it well.

G
Give her a dolly that laughs and cries,

C   G   D7   G
One that will open and shut her eyes.

Chorus 2   *Repeat Chorus 1*

Verse 3

G
Look in the stocking of little Will,

C   G   D7
Oh, just see what a glorious fill!

G
Here is a hammer and lots of tacks,

C   G   D7   G
Whistle and ball and a whip that cracks.

Chorus 3   *Repeat Chorus 1*

Wassail Song

Traditional English Carol

Here we come a - was - sail - ing...

G   D7   C   Am7   E7

Verse 1

    G   **D7**   **G**   **D7**
Here we come a-wassail-ing

     G   **D7**   **G**
A - mong the leaves so green.

C   **G**   **D7**
Here we come a wand'ring,

    Am7   **D7**
So fair to be seen.

Chorus 1

       G C   **G**
Love and joy come to you,

D7   **G**   **C**   **G**
And to you glad Christmas too.

D7   **G**   **E7**   **Am7 D7** **G**   **C**
And God bless you and send you a happy New Year,

      G   **E7** **Am7 D7**   **G**
And God send you a hap - py New Year.

UKULELE CHORD SONGBOOK

Verse 2

```
G      D7     G      D7
We are not dai - ly beg - gars

   G      D7     G
That beg from door to door

C      G              D7
But we are neighbor children

       Am7              D7
Whom you have seen be-fore.
```

Chorus 2   *Repeat Chorus 1*

Verse 3

```
G      D7  G  D7
We have got a little purse

  G         D7     G
Of stretching leather skin.

C         G   D7
We want a little money

    Am7            D7
To line it well with - in:
```

Chorus 3   *Repeat Chorus 1*

Verse 4

```
    G      D7     G    D7
God bless the master of this house,

    G      D7     G
Like-wise the mistress too;

    C     G   D7
And all the little children

       Am7            D7
That 'round the table go:
```

Chorus 4   *Repeat Chorus 1*

Watchman, Tell Us of the Night

Words by John Bowring
Music by Jacob Hintze

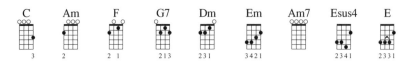

Verse 1

      C   Am C F G7   C
Watchman, tell us of the night,

          Dm C G7   C
What its signs of promise are.

      Am C   F   G7   C
Trav'ler, o'er yon mountain's height,

          Dm   C G7   C
See that glo - ry beaming star.

G7   C   Em Am7 D7   G
Watchman, does its beau - teous ray

Dm   Am Esus4 E   Am
Aught of joy or hope fore-tell?

C   F   G Am7 D7 G
Trav'ler, yes, it brings the day,

F   C   Dm C G7   C
Prom-ised day of Isra - el.

Verse 2

```
        C    Am C F G7   C
```
Watchman, tell us of the night,

```
          Dm C  G7     C
```
Higher yet that star as-cends.

```
        Am C    F  G7      C
```
Trav'ler, bless-ed-ness and light,

```
            Dm   C G7        C
```
Peace and truth, its course por-tends.

```
   G7        C  Em Am7 D7 G
```
Watchman, will its beams a - lone

```
   Dm     Am     Esus4 E   Am
```
Gild the spot that gave them birth!

```
   C       F  G  Am7 D7 G
```
Trav'ler, a - ges are_ its_ own;

```
   F   C Dm   C  G7    C
```
See it bursts o'er all the earth.

Verse 3

```
        C    Am  C F G7    C
```
Watchman, tell us of the night,

```
          Dm   C  G7     C
```
For the morn-ing seems to dawn.

```
         Am C   F   G7     C
```
Trav'ler, dark-ness takes its flight,

```
           Dm C  G7      C
```
Doubt and ter-ror are with-drawn.

```
   G7        C Em Am7 D7  G
```
Watchman, let thy wand'rings cease,

```
   Dm     Am  Esus4 E  Am
```
Hie thee to thy qui - et home.

```
   C        F  G  Am7 D7 G
```
Trav'ler, lo, the Prince of Peace,

```
   F   C  Dm  C G7    C
```
Lo, the Son of God is come.
```
```

We Are Singing

Traditional Venezuelan Folk Carol

Sing-ing, we are sing - ing...

Chorus 1

      D   **A**
Singing, we are singing

      D   **A D**
Loving praise we bring,

             G
Merry eve of Christmas,

A7   **D**
Merry eve of Christmas,

       A7 D G
Merry eve of Christmas,

A7   **D**
To Thee, Infant King.

Verse 1

      D   **Em G**
All our expec - ta - tion,

Em   **A7**   **D**
All our chari-ty,

            Em
All our conso - lation,

A7   **D**
Child dear in Thee.

Chorus 2   *Repeat Chorus 1*

Verse 2

D   Em G
Beaming through the dark-ness,

Em   A7   D
Flooding rays so bright,

            Em
Shining on the cradle,

A7   D
On the glorious night.

Chorus 3   *Repeat Chorus 1*

Verse 3

D   Em G
Night of cele - bra - tion,

Em   A7   D
Night of Jesus' birth,

            Em
Night of holy splendor,

A7   D
And redeeming love.

Chorus 4   *Repeat Chorus 1*

We Three Kings of Orient Are

Words and Music by
John H. Hopkins, Jr.

Melody:

We three kings of O - ri - ent are;...

Em	B7	D	G	Am	D7	C
3 4 2 1	3 2 1	1 2 2	1 3 2	2	1 1 1 2	3

Verse 1

   Em   B7 Em
We three kings of Orient are;

       B7   Em
Bearing gifts we traverse a-far,

     D   G
Field and fountain, moor and mountain,

Am B7 Em
Following yonder star.

Chorus 1

D7 G   C G
O___ star of wonder, star of night,

      C   G
Star with royal beauty bright,

Em D   C   D
Westward leading, still pro-ceeding,

G   C G
Guide us to thy perfect light.

Verse 2

   Em   B7   Em
Born a King on Bethlehem's plain,

       B7   Em
Gold I bring to crown Him a-gain,

     D G
King for-ever, ceasing never

Am B7 Em
Over us all to reign.

Chorus 2	*Repeat Chorus 1*

Verse 3

Em   B7   Em
Frankincense to offer have I;

                B7   Em
Incense owns a Deity nigh;

              D   G
Prayer and praising, all men raising,

Am   B7   Em
Worship Him, God most high.

Chorus 3   *Repeat Chorus 1*

Verse 4

Em   B7   Em
Myrrh is mine; its bitter per-fume

                B7   Em
Breathes a life of gathering gloom;

              D   G
Sorr'wing, sighing, bleeding, dying,

Am   B7   Em
Sealed in the stone-cold tomb.

Chorus 4   *Repeat Chorus 1*

Verse 5

Em   B7   Em
Glorious now, be-hold Him a-rise,

                B7   Em
King and God and sacri-fice,

              D G
Alle-luia, alleluia,

Am   B7   Em
Earth to hea-v'n re-plies.

Chorus 5   *Repeat Chorus 1*

We Wish You a Merry Christmas

Traditional English Folksong

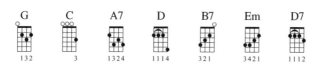

G	C	A7	D	B7	Em	D7
132	3	1324	1114	321	3421	1112

Chorus 1

       G   **C**
We wish you a merry Christmas,

   A7   **D**
We wish you a merry Christmas,

   B7   **Em**
We wish you a merry Christmas,

     C   **D7** **G**
And a happy New Year.

Verse 1

         G   D   A7   D
Good tidings we bring to you and your kin.

G   D7   G   C   D7 G
Good tidings for Christmas and a happy New Year.

Chorus 2

         G   C
We all know that Santa's coming,

         A7   D
We all know that Santa's coming,

         B7   Em
We all know that Santa's coming,

         C   D7 G
And soon will be here.

Verse 2   *Repeat Verse 1*

Chorus 3   *Repeat Chorus 1*

Welsh Carol

Words by Pastor K.E. Roberts
Traditional Welsh Carol

Melody:

A - wake were they on - ly,...

Am   E7   Dm6   Dm   G7   C   G   E

Verse 1

      Am   E7   Am
A-wake were they on - ly,

E7   Am   Dm6 Dm
Those shepherds so lone - ly,

E7 Am   E7 Am   E7   Am
On guard in that si - lence pro - found,

E7   Am   E7   Am
When color had fad - ed,

E7   Am   Dm6 Dm
When nighttime had shad - ed

E7   Am   E7 Am E7   Am
Their senses from sight and from sound.

Chorus 1

G7 C   G
Lo, then broke a won - der,

Am E   Am   E
Then drift-ed asun-der

     Am   E Am   Dm6 Am E
The veils from the splen - dor__ of__ God,

       Am   E7 Am
When light from the Ho - ly,

E7   Am   Dm6 Dm
Came down to the low - ly,

E7 Am   E7   Am E7 Am
And heav'n to the earth that they trod.

G7 C   G
O,_ spirit all-know - ing,

Am E   Am   E
Thou source overflow - ing,

   Am   E Am Dm6 Am E
O move in the dark-ness_ a - round,

     Am   E7 Am
That sight may be in_ us,

E7   Am   Dm6 Dm
True hearing to win_ us,

E7 Am   E7   Am E7 Am
Glad tidings where Christ may be found.

Verse 2

     Am   E7 Am
May light now en-fold us,

E7 Am   Dm6 Dm
O_ Lord, for be - hold_ us,

E7 Am   E7 Am E7   Am
Like shepherds from tu - mult with - drawn,

E7 Am   E7   Am
Nor heaving, nor see - ing,

E7 Am   Dm6 Dm
All other care flee - ing,

E7 Am   E7 Am E7 Am
We wait the in - eff - a - ble dawn.

Chorus 2   *Repeat Chorus 1*

What Child Is This?

Words by William C. Dix
16th Century English Melody

Em   D   C   B7   Bm   G

Verse 1

     Em   **D**
What Child is this, who, laid to rest,

    C   **B7**
On Mary's lap is sleeping?

      Em   **D**
Whom angels greet with anthems sweet,

     C   **B7**   **Em**
While shepherds watch are keeping?

Chorus 1

Bm G   **D**   **Bm**
This, this is Christ the King,

      Em   **C**   **B7**
Whom shepherds guard and angels sing:

G   **D**   **Bm**
Haste, haste to bring Him laud,

     Em   **B7** **Em**
The Babe, the Son of Mary.

Verse 2

Em   D
Why lies He in such mean estate

C   B7
Where ox and ass are feeding?

Em   D
Good Christian, fear, for sinners here

C   B7   Em
The silent Word is pleading.

Chorus 2   *Repeat Chorus 1*

Verse 3

Em   D
So bring Him incense, gold, and myrrh,

C   B7
Come peasant king to own Him;

Em   D
The King of kings sal-vation brings,

C   B7   Em
Let loving hearts en-throne Him.

Chorus 3   *Repeat Chorus 1*

When Christ Was Born of Mary Free

Music by Arthur H. Brown
Traditional Text, 15th Century

Melody:

When Christ was born of __ Mar - y __ free,...

G	D	Bm	Em	Am	D7	A7	Dm	C	Am7
1 3 2	1 1 1 4	3 1 1 1	3 4 2 1	1	1 1 1 2	1 3 2 4	2 3 1	3	

Verse 1

G   D   Bm Em   Am D7 G
When Christ was born of Mar - y free,

   D7   G   Em A7 D
In Bethle-hem that fair cit - y,

   Dm   Am   C   G
An - gels sung there with mirth and glee:

   D7   G
"In excelsis glori - a."

Chorus 1

G   C   G
In excelsis glori - a,

D   Am7 D7 G D7 G
In ex - cel - sis glo - ri - a,

   Em C G Am D
In ex - cel - sis glo - ri - a.

G   Em G D7 G
In excel-sis glo - ri - a.

Verse 2

G   D   Bm Em   Am D7 G
This King is_ come to save man-kind,

  D7   G   Em A7 D
As in the scripture truths we find,

     Dm   Am   C   G
There-fore this song we have in mind:

       D7   G
"In excelsis glori - a."

Chorus 2

Repeat Chorus 1

Verse 3

G   D   Bm Em   Am D7 G
Then, dear-est Lord, for Thy great grace,

  D7 G   Em A7 D
Grant us in bliss to see Thy face,

    Dm   Am   C   G
That we may sing to Thy so-lace:

     D7   G
"In excelsis glori - a."

Chorus 3

Repeat Chorus 1

Whence Comes This Rush of Wings

Traditional French Carol

Whence comes this rush of wings a - far,...

Am   G   C   Em   B7   Dm   E7

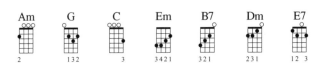

Verse 1

Am   G   C   G
Whence comes this rush of wings a-far,

Am   G   Am Em B7 Em
Following straight the No - ël_ star?

Am   G   C   G
Birds from the woods in wondrous flight,

C   Dm Am E7 Am
Bethlehem seek this ho - ly night.

Verse 2

Am   G   C   G
"Tell us, ye birds, why come ye here,

Am   G Am Em B7   Em
Into this sta-ble_ poor and drear?"

Am   G   C   G
"Hast'ning we seek the Newborn King,

C   Dm Am E7 Am
And all our sweet-est mu - sic bring."

Verse 3

Am   G   C   G
Hark how the green finch bears his part,

Am   G Am Em B7 Em
Philomel, too, with ten - der heart

Am   G   C   G
Chants from her leafy dark re-treat,

C   Dm Am E7 Am
"Re mi fa sol" in__ ac - cents sweet.

Verse 4

Am   G   C   G
Angels and shepherds, birds of the sky,

Am   G Am Em B7 Em
Come where the Son of__ God doth lie.

Am   G   C   G
Christ on earth with man doth dwell,

C   Dm Am E7 Am
Join in the shout, "No - ël, No - ël."

While by My Sheep

Traditional German Carol

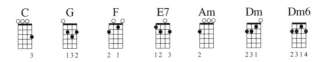

C   G   F   E7   Am   Dm   Dm6

Verse 1

    C   G F C   F   G C
While by my sheep I watched at night,

    G F   C   F G C
Glad tid-ings brought an an-gel bright.

Chorus 1

    E7   Am E7   Am
How great my joy, great my joy.

    G C Am G C
Joy, joy, joy, joy, joy, joy!

    Dm   E7 F Dm6 E7 Am
Praise to the Lord in heav'n on high.

UKULELE CHORD SONGBOOK

Verse 2

```
C    G   F C     F G C
```
There shall be born, so he did say,

```
G   F C    F   G C
```
In Beth-le-hem, a Child to - day.

Chorus 2   *Repeat Chorus 1*

Verse 3

```
C   G   F C    F   G C
```
There shall He lie, in man-ger mean,

```
G   F C     F   G   C
```
Who shall re-deem the world from sin.

Chorus 3   *Repeat Chorus 1*

Verse 4

```
C    G F C     F  G C
```
Lord, ev-er-more to me be nigh,

```
G   F  C    F   G   C
```
Then shall my heart be filled with joy!

Chorus 4   *Repeat Chorus 1*

While Shepherds Watched Their Flocks

Words by Nahum Tate
Music by George Frideric Handel

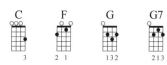

Verse 1

         C   **F**   **C**
While shepherds watched their flocks by night,

            G
All seated on the ground,

   G7   **C**
The angel of the Lord came down,

   F   **G7**   **C**
And glory shone a-round.

Verse 2

         C   **F**   **C**
"Fear not," said he, for mighty dread

               G
Had seized their troubled mind.

   G7   **C**
"Glad tidings of great joy I bring

   F   **G7**   **C**
To you and all man-kind.

UKULELE CHORD SONGBOOK

Verse 3

```
        C     F     C
"To you in David's town this day
                G
Is born of David's line
   G7           C
A Savior, who is Christ the Lord,
      F     G7    C
And this shall be the sign.
```

Verse 4

```
        C     F     C
"The heav'nly babe you there shall find
                G
To human view dis-played,
   G7                C
All meanly wrapped in swathing bands
      F   G7      C
And in a manger laid."
```

Verse 5

```
        C      F     C
Thus spoke the seraph, and forthwith
                G
Appeared a shining throng
   G7           C
Of angels praising God on high,
      F     G7        C
Who thus ad-dressed their song:
```

Verse 6

```
        C    F    C
"All glory be to God on high,
                G
And on the earth be peace;
   G7                C
Good-will henceforth from heav'n to earth
      F     G7   C
Be-gin and never cease!"
```

Yuletide Is Here Again

Traditional Swedish Dance Carol

Melody:

Yule - tide is here a - gain,...

G   C   D7

132   3   1112

Verse 1

    G
Yuletide is here again,

The yuletide is here again,

Let's celebrate, rejoice till Easter.

C
Then when it's Eastertime,

    G
Yes, then, when it's Eastertime,

    D7   **G**
We'll celebrate, rejoice till Christ-mas.

Verse 2

    G
Yuletide is here again,

The yuletide is here again,

Let's celebrate, rejoice till Easter.

C   **G**
Ev'ryone knows this really cannot be so,

    D7   **G**
Because of Lent, when we all must start fast-ing.